COUTURE
wedding cakes

Mich Turner
of Little Venice Cake Company

COUTURE
wedding cakes

photography by
RICHARD JUNG

jacqui
small

For Phil, Marlow and George –
my shining stars

First published in 2009 by
Jacqui Small LLP
7 Greenland Street
London NW1 0ND

Publisher Jacqui Small
Editorial Manager Lesley Felce
Art Director Maggie Town
Designer Beverly Price
Additional Photography Janine Hosegood,
Sarah Cuttle
Editor Alison Bolus
Production Peter Colley

ISBN 978 1 906417 07 9

A catalogue record for this book is available
from the British Library.

2010 2009 2008
10 9 8 7 6 5 4 3 2 1

Printed in China

CONTENTS

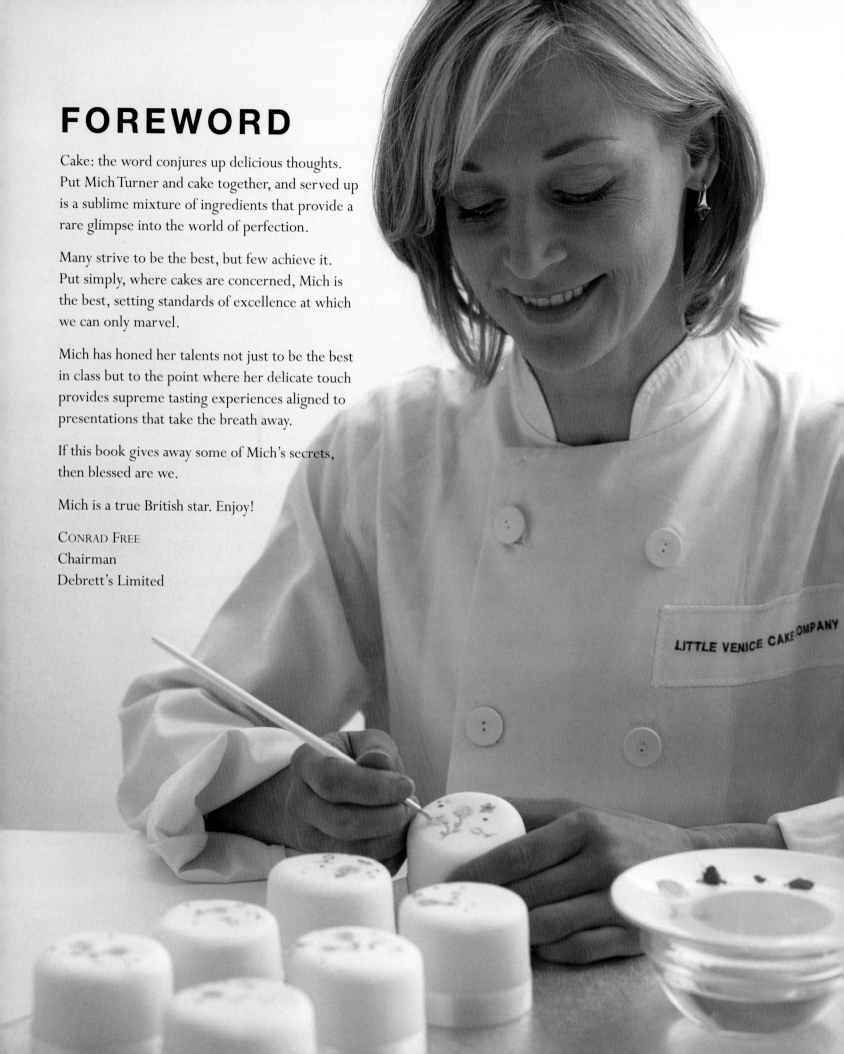

FOREWORD

Cake: the word conjures up delicious thoughts.
Put Mich Turner and cake together, and served up
is a sublime mixture of ingredients that provide a
rare glimpse into the world of perfection.

Many strive to be the best, but few achieve it.
Put simply, where cakes are concerned, Mich is
the best, setting standards of excellence at which
we can only marvel.

Mich has honed her talents not just to be the best
in class but to the point where her delicate touch
provides supreme tasting experiences aligned to
presentations that take the breath away.

If this book gives away some of Mich's secrets,
then blessed are we.

Mich is a true British star. Enjoy!

CONRAD FREE
Chairman
Debrett's Limited

INTRODUCTION

I was privileged and honoured to be named the *Harper's Bazaar* and Chanel Entrepreneur of the Year in 2006. One element of my prize was a personal shopping experience with Chanel in London's Old Bond Street. I was afforded the full red-carpet treatment: Champagne on arrival and a personal showcase of the entire collection. I bounced out of the store three hours later with a tailor-made iconic Chanel tweed jacket, a string of pearls and a bottle of Coco Chanel perfume…and so began my love affair with haute couture.

Since then I have become fascinated by all elements of fashion, using them as sources of inspiration for new wedding cake designs: from the glamorous Tiller Girls at the turn of the 20th century, and the elegant simplicity of Coco Chanel of the 1930s; through the early days of Karl Lagerfeld and Yves Saint Laurent at the House of Christian Dior in Paris in the 1950s; to modern-day fun and funky Galliano and Christian Lacroix and the more romantic and contemporary Elie Saab, Matthew Williamson and Amanda Wakeley.

If the thought of making a wedding cake seems rather daunting, look closely at many of the cakes here and you will see that some are actually quite simple – three tiers stacked or blocked, with minimal decoration – but stunning just the same. A pure white cake with contrasting ribbon trim can be just as eye-catching as a flower-festooned creation. So be inspired: these are all tried-and-tested designs that really do work, and the cake recipes, ranging from traditional fruit and ever-popular sticky date to more unusual lime and coconut, are delicious.

Mich Turner

setting the scene

THE MAIN ATTRACTION

Cutting the cake is the first official role of the new bride, and as such it is imperative that the cake is displayed to best effect. The cake should be clearly visible to the guests, provide the perfect setting for a photo opportunity and be accessible to both the bride and groom and venue waiting staff.

The idea of the wedding cake dates back to Roman times, when the groom would break a loaf of bread over the bride's head to symbolize prosperity, longevity and fertility. Later, guests at medieval weddings were known to bring small cakes to a wedding banquet and pile these together on a table to create a stack of cakes over which the bride and groom had to try to kiss each other. This stack of small cakes later evolved into the multi-tiered wedding cake we have today. An important figure in the development of the tiered wedding cake was a baker named William Rich, who was based in Fleet Street, London, in the 19th century. He created a wedding cake for his daughter based on the octagonal steeple of St Bride's Church in Fleet Street.

The use of a rich fruit cake baked with vine fruits steeped in brandy for a wedding cake came to symbolize wealth, fertility, happiness, longevity and health, and its keeping properties made it ideal as designs became more complicated and so took longer to decorate. As for the white icing, this was made from costly fine sugar, which meant that only the wealthy could afford to use it. Its use became fashionable after Queen Victoria set the trend of marrying in white. Nowadays the wedding cake – now available in every shade and hue of colour, and varying from chic and simple to complex and extravagant – is an important and integral part of the wedding along with the wedding dress and the bride's bouquet.

"The wedding cake should be centre stage at the reception – a star in its own right."

opposite *Venetian presented on a round silver cake stand in front of the marble stone fireplace at the little-known 30 Pavilion Road in Knightsbridge. The cake's blocked roses are complemented by tea lights and the bridal bouquet.*

below *Queen Elizabeth Diamond on display in the ballroom foyer at Claridge's. The five-tier cake, displayed on a bed of yellow-toned flowers, takes centre stage, welcoming guests as they enter the ballroom by passing through the revolving doors and up the staircase.*

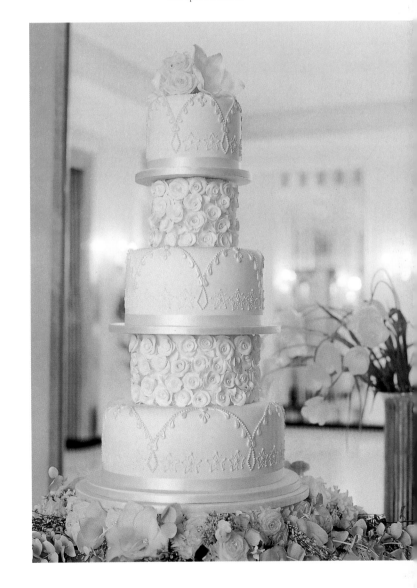

WHERE TO PUT THE CAKE When setting the scene to create the perfect backdrop for the wedding cake, the most important consideration is location. Whether the cake takes centre stage in a grand ballroom, is framed by a beautiful fireplace or is positioned by a sweeping staircase, it is important to think about the ideal time for cutting the cake so it can be presented to best effect within the venue.

The cake should be presented in a prominent position that is easily accessible to the bride and groom and has a pleasing background to ensure a natural photo opportunity. For a more intimate occasion, consider positioning the wedding cake as a centrepiece on the main wedding breakfast table.

Wedding cakes are often presented on the dance floor. Whilst this can create a seemingly perfect space to showcase the cake, caution should be taken if the dance floor is sprung or if the guests will be invited to dance between courses, as this can make the cake unstable. Similarly, wedding cakes may be set up in a marquee, but the ground is rarely level and stable, and for these locations I would strongly advise against a multi-tiered wedding cake separated with pillars, columns or flowers – opt instead for a stacked cake, which will be better supported.

opposite Spring Rain set up on the main wedding breakfast table in the Penthouse of The Dorchester. The cake is on view for all the guests to admire at this intimate wedding.

below Spring Phalaenopsis *Orchid* presented on a white porcelain stand at the base of a sweeping staircase – a natural spot for the bride and groom to cut the cake.

> *"Use flowers, candles and lighting to ensure the cake is the star of the reception."*

opposite Pearlique is set on a stunningly simple silver-effect cake stand fully dressed with fresh flowers and delicate tea lights.

right Amaryllis Pearl is presented on a mirrored Perspex disc dressed with fresh blooms in dramatically contrasting colours to create balance and harmony.

below Summer Basket Weave is nestled on a garland of fresh flowers and foliage to lift the wedding cake and carry the theme of the flowers through to the bouquet on top.

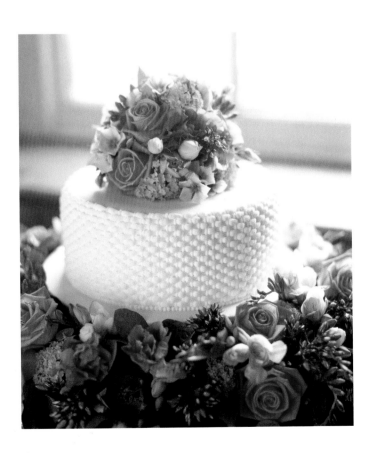

Wedding cakes can be displayed on a clothed service trolley, which can be wheeled from the centre of the dance floor into the kitchen for cutting, or simply laid on a polished wooden table. Tables do not have to be clothed, but fine linens or sumptuous fabrics can certainly enhance and complement a wedding cake. Damask cloths in shades of ivory add glamour, whilst coloured silks can be more fun and funky. Alternatively, create a topiary tablecloth by studding it with fresh flowers.

FLOWERS AND CANDLES Flowers and candles can greatly enhance and complement the table setting for the cake. A silver cake stand can be fully dressed with an abundance of fresh scented flowers; alternatively, stud a polystyrene plinth base with fresh flowers and nestle the wedding cake on top to create a floral garland. Candles should not be positioned too close to the cake, otherwise there is a danger of melting it or singeing the flowers (or even the bride and groom as they cut the cake). Ideally, the cake should be spot-lit from above for maximum effect.

CAKE STANDS AND KNIVES

The cake on its base board can be set directly onto a table, but there are also a number of options with more dramatic effect. The most popular choice is a polished solid silver square or round cake stand, which can show off a wedding cake simply and elegantly. Beautiful etched glass stands also look stunning, as do solid silver salvers. All of these stands can be used for dinner parties and afternoon teas long after the wedding day is over, so the bride might consider buying a stand rather than hiring it from the wedding venue.

Cube vases filled with flowers, pea lights or coloured water set together as bricks can be a fun method of presenting a cake, while mirrored Perspex discs laid on a polystyrene block of fresh flowers add drama. Monochrome designs, such as Ascot Pearl, would be complemented by black or white china stands.

For a multi-tiered wedding cake, it is advisable to cut the cake with a proper cake knife, often known as a bride's knife. There are many styles available, including silver, gold, glass-handled and bone-handled. If the knife is bought rather than hired, it could be engraved with the names of the bride and groom and the date of the wedding. It can then be kept and passed down through the family as a cherished heirloom. Another choice is to use a dramatic silver sword, such as a reproduction Scottish claymore, which could also be engraved to commemorate the day.

An ornate cake slice would be more appropriate if the wedding cake will be served as a dessert.

Traditionally, the bride and groom are invited to cut the cake after the formal speeches have been made at the end of the wedding breakfast.

opposite A collection of cake knives and servers in a variety of sizes and styles, both plain and decorative, and some with contrasting handles for interest.

right A selection of cake stands, clockwise from top right: round solid silver cake stand with Little Venice Lace; etched glass cake stand with Vintage Rose Crown; solid silver shell and scroll salver with Sea Pearls; white porcelain cake stand with Parisian Pearl; square silver-effect cake stand with Bows and Brooches; black lacquered cake stand with Ascot Pearl.

CUTTING THE CAKE

The bride puts her right hand on the knife, then the groom puts his hand on top of hers with his other arm around her waist. The bride then grasps the knife gently with her left hand, so showing off her ring.

With a tiered cake, it is always the base tier that is cut and served; the bride can then cut a small taster and feed it to her husband. With stands of individual cakes, there may be a larger top tier to cut. Rather than attempt to cut all the way through this tier, which could make the stand unstable, the couple should just pose with the knife, and the bride can cut a taster piece from one of the small cakes with a pastry fork.

For a less formal celebration or Champagne reception, it can be appropriate to set the cake table with Champagne glasses and linen napkins. The bride and groom can make a Champagne toast by the cake and seal it with a kiss.

above A decorated Autumnal Candy Stripe individually presented with a Champagne tea. The classic, low-key tableware provides the perfect setting for these elaborate little cakes.

right A generous slice of wedding cake served on a highly decorative plate with a pastry fork for ease of eating. The cake can be accompanied by a cup of tea and glass of chilled Champagne.

opposite The bride and groom cutting the base tier of the wedding cake. It is traditional for the bride to feed the first mouthful to her new husband.

glamorous

QUEEN ELIZABETH DIAMOND

I designed this cake to celebrate the Diamond Wedding anniversary of HRH Queen Elizabeth II and Prince Philip in 2007. The pearl design is repeated six times around each tier, one for each decade of marriage. The tiers are separated by columns of white sugar roses and leaves, studded with Swarovski crystals.

YOU WILL NEED

20cm (8in), 30cm (12in) and 40cm (16in) round cakes

2 x 20cm (8in), 30cm (12in) and 40cm (16in) thin round cake boards, for the cakes

20cm (8in), 30cm (12in) and 40cm (16in) round polystyrene dummies 7.5cm (3in) deep, for the tiers

8.65kg (19lb) marzipan, for the cakes

21.6kg (47lb 8oz) sugar paste – 12kg (26lb 7oz) for the cakes, 4.35kg (9lb 8oz) for the boards, 2.25kg (5lb) for the columns and 3kg (6lb 9oz) for the roses and leaves

28cm (11in), 38cm (15in), 50cm (20in) and 55cm (22in) thick round cake boards

2 quantities royal icing (see page 133)

5.45m (6 yards) ribbon 15mm (⅝in) wide, cut into 90cm (36in), 1.2m (48in), 1.6m (63in) and 1.75m (69in) lengths

glue stick

15cm (6in) and 25cm (10in) round polystyrene dummies 12cm (5in) deep, for the columns

15cm (6in) and 25cm (10in) thin round cake boards, for the columns

sharp knife

tracing paper and pen

scribe

2cm (¾in) rose-leaf plunger veiner and cutter

5 piping bags

nos. 1.5, 2, 3 and 4 icing nozzles

30g (1oz) topaz lustre

3 tbsp edible gel

paintbrush

3m (3¼ yards) ribbon 25mm (1in) wide, cut into 65cm (26in), 1m (39in) and 1.3m (52in) lengths

sharp scissors

20 white 28-gauge wires, cut into 3

60 Swarovski 10mm (⅜in) bicone crystal beads

16 dowels

1 Place the 20cm (8in) cake on a thin board, then on a shallow polystyrene dummy and then on a second thin board, all of the same size. Repeat using the 30cm (12in) and 40cm (16in) cakes, thin boards and dummies. Cover each column with a layer of marzipan (1.3kg/ 3lb, 2.75kg/6lb and 4.6kg/10lb respectively) and sugar paste (2.15kg/4lb 12oz, 3.85kg/ 8lb 7oz and 6kg/13lb 4oz respectively), following the techniques on pages 128 and 130–1. Cover the thick cake boards (the base boards) with sugar paste (see pages 130–1 for quantities and technique). Leave the columns and boards to firm overnight.

2 Put a dab of royal icing on the largest base board, then place the other base board centrally on top. Position the bottom tier centrally on the stacked boards, again using icing, then attach the other 2 tiers to the 2 remaining boards. Fix a length of 15mm (⅝in) ribbon around all 4 boards using a glue stick.

3 Fix the deep polystyrene dummies onto thin cake boards of the same size with icing. Roll 750g (1lb 10oz) sugar paste into a 12 x 50cm (5 x 20in) piece for the 15cm (6in) dummy and 1.5kg (3¼lb) sugar paste into a 12 x 80cm (5 x 32in) piece for the 25cm (10in) dummy. Wet the dummies and roll over the paste to fix. Trim and leave to firm.

4 Trace the designs from the templates on pages 153, 156 and 157 and scribe them onto the relevant tiers 6 times. Make 140 hand-moulded roses, following the technique on page 136, and 60 rose leaves of varying sizes (3.5cm/1⅜in, 5cm/2in and 6cm/2⅜in) using the leaf cutter and veiner, following the technique on page 110.

5 Fit 4 of the piping bags with the icing nozzles and fill with royal icing. Begin with no. 4 for the main pearl drops and diamanté drops. Then use no. 3 for the pearls above this line, no. 2 for the larger pearls and drops inside each star and no. 1.5 for the smallest pearls and the outline of each star. Leave to set for 4 hours or overnight.

6 Blend the topaz lustre with half the edible gel to form a paste. Brush the main piped pearl detail with this glaze and use clear edible gel alone to glaze the stars. Wrap a length of 25mm (1in) ribbon around the base of each tier, trim neatly and fix with a dab of icing.

7 Fill the remaining piping bag with icing, snip the end off and use the icing to fix the roses and leaves in position around the columns, being careful not to go up over the top (place a larger plain cake board on top of the column as a guide).

8 Push a wire length through each of the crystals until the crystal is halfway along the wire. Bend the wire over so that the 2 halves meet under the crystal and twist to secure. Push the wired crystals between the roses into the iced columns and leave to set.

9 Dowel the base and middle tiers with 8 dowels, following the technique on page 143. Stack the cakes and columns, icing the columns to the cakes above and below for stability.

LENGTHS OF RIBBON REQUIRED (APPROX.)

Size of round tier cake	20cm (8in)	30cm (12in)	40cm (16in)	
Length of ribbon	70cm (28in)	1m (39in)	1.3m (52in)	
Size of round board	28cm (11in)	38cm (15in)	50cm (20in)	55cm (22in)
Length of ribbon	90cm (36in)	1.2m (48in)	1.6m (63in)	1.75m (69in)

QUANTITIES OF MARZIPAN AND SUGAR PASTE REQUIRED

Size of cake	20cm (8in)	30cm (12in)	40cm (16in)
Quantity of marzipan	1.3kg (3lb)	2.75kg (6lb)	4.6kg (10lb)
Quantity of sugar paste	2.15kg (4lb 13oz)	3.85kg (8lb 6oz)	6kg (13lb)
Size of column	15cm (6in)	25cm (10in)	
Quantity of marzipan	–	–	
Quantity of sugar paste	750g (1lb 10oz)	1.5kg (3lb 5oz)	

LITTLE VENICE LACE™ *This is our iconic Little Venice*

Cake Company design, which was inspired by luxurious silk and velvet flocking.
I did feature a single, heart-shaped cake of this design for intimate weddings in
my previous book, Fantastic Party Cakes, but for a wedding cake with more impact
and breathtaking beauty, try four tiers!

YOU WILL NEED

15cm (6in), 23cm (9in), 30cm (12in) and
38cm (15in) round cakes

15cm (6in), 23cm (9in), 30cm (12in) and
38cm (15in) thin round cake boards

marzipan, for the cakes
(see page 129 for quantities)

ivory sugar paste, for the cakes and boards
(see pages 130 and 131 for quantities)

23cm (9in), 30cm (12in), 38cm (15in) and
45cm (18in) thick round cake boards

4.4m (4¾ yards) ivory ribbon 15mm (⅝in) wide,
cut into 75cm (30in), 1m (39in), 1.2m (48in) and
1.45m (57in) lengths

glue stick

tracing paper and pen

scribe

piping bag

no. 2 icing nozzle

1½ quantities royal icing (see page 133),
coloured with concentrated ivory edible food colour

3.45m (3¾ yards) ivory ribbon 12mm (½in) wide,
cut into 50cm (20in), 75cm (30in), 1m (39in) and
1.2m (48in) lengths

sharp scissors

12 dowels

10cm (4in), 18cm (7in) and 25cm (10in)
polystyrene columns 5cm (2in) deep

27 floristry wires, cut into 3

3 heads of white hydrangea and 80 Bianca roses

1 Place the cakes on thin cake boards of the same size and cover with marzipan and ivory sugar paste, following the techniques on pages 128 and 130–1. Cover the thick cake boards (the base boards) with sugar paste, following the technique on page 130. Fix a length of 15mm (⅝in) ribbon around the edge of each base board using a glue stick. Leave the cakes and boards to firm overnight, then place each cake on its base board. Trace the design from the template on page 154 and scribe it onto each tier of the cake.

2 Fit the piping bag with the icing nozzle and fill with ivory royal icing. Pipe the design onto the cake. Wrap a length of 12mm (½in) ribbon around the base of each tier, trim neatly and hold in position with a dab of icing.

3 Block the tiers with the flowers, following the technique on page 140. Dress the top tier to finish.

VENETIAN

I particularly like this sophisticated combination of ivory, caramel and taupe. The design was inspired by traditional Venetian glass etchings on gorgeous stemware. The combination of the detailed icing and sumptuous roses creates a cake that is quite regal and suitable for a more formal wedding celebration.

YOU WILL NEED

15cm (6in), 20cm (8in) and 25cm (10in) round cakes

15cm (6in), 20cm (8in) and 25cm (10in) thin round cake boards

marzipan, for the cakes (see page 129 for quantities)

ivory sugar paste, for the cakes and boards (see pages 130 and 131 for quantities)

23cm (9in), 28cm (11in) and 33cm (13in) thick round cake boards

2.75m (3 yards) caramel ribbon 15mm (⅝in) wide, cut into 75cm (30in), 90cm (36in) and 1.1m (44in) lengths

glue stick

tracing paper and pen

scribe

2 piping bags

nos. 1.5 and 2 icing nozzles

1 quantity royal icing (see page 133) coloured with concentrated taupe edible food colour

1.95m (2¼ yards) caramel ribbon 12mm (½in) wide, cut into 50cm (20in), 65cm (26in) and 80cm (32in) lengths

sharp scissors

10cm (4in) and 15cm (6in) polystyrene columns 5cm (2in) deep

8 dowels

14 Metallica roses and 14 Vandella roses, for the tiers, plus extra for the top

12 floristry wires, cut into 3

2.8m (3 yards) dark brown ribbon 15mm (⅝in) wide, cut into 20cm (8in) lengths

1 Place the cakes on thin cake boards of the same size and cover with marzipan and ivory sugar paste, following the techniques on pages 128 and 130–1. Cover the thick cake boards (the base boards) with ivory sugar paste, following the technique on page 130. Fix lengths of 15mm (⅝in) caramel ribbon around the base boards using a glue stick. Leave the cakes and boards to firm overnight.

2 Trace the design from the template on pages 152–3 and scribe it onto each tier of the cake.

3 Fit the piping bags with the icing nozzles and fill with taupe royal icing. Use no. 2 to pipe the hearts and larger pearls of the design and no.1.5 to fill in all the smaller pearls and the leaf garlands. Wrap a length of 12mm (½in) caramel ribbon around the base of each tier, trim neatly and hold in position with a dab of royal icing.

4 Block the tiers with the flowers, following the technique on page 140. Tie the lengths of 15mm (⅝in) brown ribbon around half of the roses (close to the calyx) and trim the ribbon ends to points with sharp scissors. When fixing the roses into the columns, intersperse the beribboned and plain roses, so the ribbons peep out between the flowers. Dress the top tier to finish.

AMARYLLIS PEARL

The refined opulence of the Art Deco era was the inspiration for this cake, with its combination of jet black, pure white and regal purple. The tiers are of different depths and are presented on a mirrored plate set on a bed of fresh flowers, including some stunning Mont Blanc amaryllis blooms.

YOU WILL NEED

15cm (6in) and 25cm (10in) round cakes, and a half-depth 20cm (8in) round cake

15cm (6in), 25cm (10in) and 33cm (13in) thin round cake boards, plus a 15cm (6in) thin board to scribe around

20cm (8in) thick round cake board

marzipan, to cover the cakes (see page 129 for quantities)

sugar paste, to cover the cakes and base board (see pages 130 and 131 for quantities)

2.65m (8ft 6in) purple ribbon 15mm (⅝in) wide

sharp scissors

1 quantity royal icing (see page 133), divided into 3 and coloured with concentrated edible food colours as follows: ⅓ purple, ⅓ black and ⅓ left white

10cm (4in) round polystyrene column 5cm (2in) deep

glue stick

40cm (16in) round mirrored Perspex disc or plate

scribe

4 piping bags

nos 1.5, 2 (x 2) and 3 icing nozzles

10 dowels

deep violet hellebores, purple anemones, Mont Blanc amaryllis, Hot Chocolat calla lilies, viburnum berries and galax leaves

1 Place the 15cm (6in) and 25cm (10in) cakes on thin cake boards of the same size and place the half-depth 20cm (8in) cake on a thick cake board of the same size. Cover with marzipan and sugar paste, following the techniques on pages 128 and 130–1. Cover the 33cm (13in) thin board (the base board) with sugar paste, following the technique on page 130. Leave the cakes and board to firm overnight.

2 Wrap 65cm (26in) of the ribbon around the base of the second tier, trim neatly and hold in position with a dab of royal icing. Wrap the remaining ribbon around the polystyrene column and fix with a glue stick. Stack the top 2 tiers centrally, following the technique on page 141. Fix the base tier to the covered board using a dab of icing, then fix the base board and tier centrally on the mirrored disc with icing. Place the 15cm (6in) thin board centrally on top of the base tier and scribe around it, then remove the board.

3 Fit 4 piping bags with nozzles and fill with icing as follows: no. 1.5 with purple; no. 2 with white; no. 2 with black; and no. 3 with white. Starting on the top of the base tier, pipe a ring of black pearls around the scribed line. Pipe a row of white pearls with the no. 2 nozzle from every other black pearl and shorter rows of purple pearls in between, either doing all one colour then the other, or changing colour as you work around the cake.

4 Pipe rows of white pearls around the base of the base tier with the no. 3 nozzle.

5 Take the purple pearls down onto the board and mirrored disc. Pipe rows of pearls around the join between the top and middle tiers. Leave to dry.

6 Dowel the base tier following the technique on page 143. Position the central column and place the top 2 tiers in position. Dress with the fresh flowers.

TIP

This cake has been displayed on a bed of fresh flowers, using a plinth of polystyrene for support. This accentuates a smaller cake while carrying the decorative theme through.

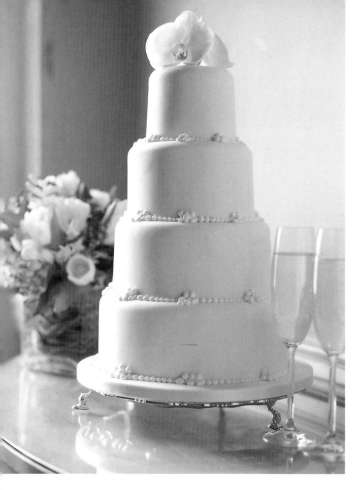

SEA PEARLS
Nautical influences have always featured in couture and fashion — with shells, scales and mermaid-tail gowns constantly being reinvented and showcasing on the catwalk. This Sea Pearls design features clusters of white glazed pearls for a simple, yet stunning, design, topped with fresh orchids.

YOU WILL NEED

10cm (4in), 15cm (6in), 20cm (8in) and 25cm (10in) round cakes

10cm (4in), 15cm (6in), 20cm (8in), 25cm (10in) and 35cm (14in) thick round cake boards

marzipan, for the cakes (see page 129 for quantities)

sugar paste, for the cakes and board (see pages 130 and 131 for quantities)

18 dowels

1.15m (1¼ yards) ribbon 15mm (⅝in) wide

glue stick

scribe

ruler

piping bag

no. 3 icing nozzle

1 quantity royal icing (see page 133)

30g (1oz) edible gel

paintbrush

3 *Phalaenopsis* orchids

1 Place the cakes on thick boards of the same size and cover with marzipan and white sugar paste, following the techniques on pages 128 and 130–1. Cover the 35cm (14in) cake board (the base board) with sugar paste, following the technique on page 130. Leave the cakes and board to firm overnight.

2 Stack the tiers centrally, following the technique on page 141, and fix the ribbon around the base board using a glue stick.

3 Use the scribe to mark out 8 points around the base of the top tier. This can be done by eye, looking down onto the cake from above. Mark north, south, east and west points, then the mid points in between. Use a ruler to continue these points vertically down over the other tiers, marking the same points on the cake board at the base of each cake.

4 Fit the piping bag with the icing nozzle and fill with royal icing. Starting at the base of the top tier, pipe a cluster of large pearls directly over one of the scribed points. Make a line of pearls along to the next marked point, descending in size as you go. When you reach the next mark, make another cluster of pearls. Repeat around the entire tier, then with the other tiers, working downwards. Leave to firm.

5 Paint edible gel on the pearls using a paintbrush to create a sparkling, sea-washed effect. Dress the cake with 3 simple *Phalaenopsis* orchids.

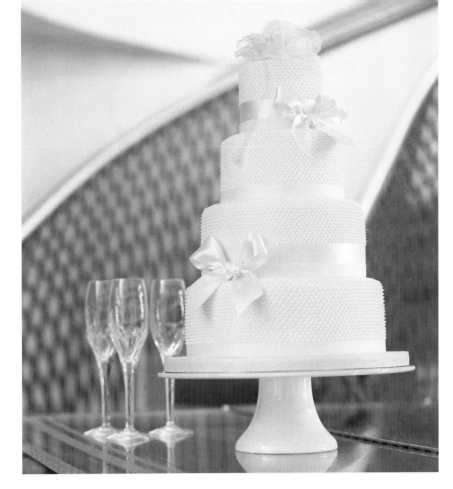

10cm (4in), 15cm (6in), 20cm (8in) and 25cm (10in)
round cakes

10cm (4in), 15cm (6in), 20cm (8in), 25cm (10in) and
33cm (13in) thick round cake boards

marzipan, for the cakes (see page 129 for quantities)

sugar paste, for the cakes and base board
(see pages 130 and 131 for quantities)

3m (3¼ yards) white double satin ribbon
35mm (1⅜in) wide, cut into 35cm (14in) and
65cm (26in) lengths; the rest for the bows

sharp scissors

1 quantity royal icing (see page 133)

3.4m (3¾ yards) white grosgrain ribbon 15mm (⅝in)
wide, cut into 35cm (14in), 50cm (20in), 65cm
(26in), 80cm (32in) and 1.1m (44in) lengths

18 dowels

glue stick

piping bag

no 1.5 icing nozzle

white silk rose

PARISIAN PEARL

Sexy and chic, my Parisian Pearl was inspired by Coco Chanel and Marlene Dietrich, with their elegant black and white couture and sophisticated cigarette holders. By using a contrasting colour ribbon behind the narrow one and for the bows (see page 34), you can personalize this design to suit any wedding.

1 Place the cakes on thick cake boards of the same size and cover with marzipan and sugar paste, following the techniques on pages 128 and 130–1. Cover the largest board (the base board) with sugar paste, following the technique on page 130. Leave the cakes and board to firm overnight.

2 Wrap a length of 35mm (1⅜in) ribbon around the base of the top and third tiers, trim neatly and hold in position with a dab of royal icing. Overlay this with lengths of 15mm (⅝in) grosgrain ribbon. On the second and base tiers, use just the 15mm (⅝in) grosgrain ribbon.

3 Stack the tiers centrally, following the technique on page 141, and fix into position on the base board with a little royal icing. Fix the remaining length of 15mm (⅝in) ribbon around the edge of the base board using a glue stick. Use the remaining 2m (2⅛ yards) of the 35mm (1⅜in) ribbon to make 2 bows and set aside.

4 Fit the piping bag with the icing nozzle and fill with royal icing. Starting with the top tier, pipe a single row of delicate pearls just above the double satin ribbon, spaced roughly 3mm (⅛in) apart. Pipe the next row above and in between the first. Repeat up the side of the tier, finishing with a neat row around the top flush with the top of the tier. Repeat with the other tiers. Leave to set overnight, then ice the 2 ribbon bows in place and put the silk rose on top.

CORSETIÈRE

I was inspired by glamorous bronze silk corsets with black lace detailing for this cake. Beautifully structured corsets can be worn in their own right (think John Paul Gaultier!) or provide the perfect shape for tailored clothes. The chocolate tiers are lustred with bronze before the intricate black pearl design is added. (See main picture on page 35.)

YOU WILL NEED

10cm (4in), 15cm (6in), 20cm (8in) and 25cm (10in) round cakes

10cm (4in), 15cm (6in), 20cm (8in), 25cm (10in) and 33cm (13in) thick round cake boards

marzipan or white chocolate plastique (see page 135), for the cakes (see page 129 for quantities)

chocolate sugar paste, for the cakes (see page 130 for quantities)

50g (2oz) bronze lustre

edible varnish spray (optional)

black sugar paste, for the base board (see page 131 for quantity)

glue stick

1.1m (44in) black double satin ribbon 15mm (⅝in) wide

tracing paper and pen

scribe

2 piping bags

nos. 1.5 and 2 icing nozzles

1 quantity royal icing (see page 133), coloured with concentrated black edible food colour

2.3m (2½ yards) black double satin ribbon 12mm (½in) wide, cut into 35cm (14in), 50cm (20in), 65cm (26in) and 80cm (32in) lengths

sharp scissors

18 dowels

silk rose

1 Place the cakes on thick cake boards of the same size and cover with marzipan or white chocolate plastique, topped with chocolate sugar paste, following the techniques on pages 128 and 130–1.

2 Using your fingers, rub bronze lustre over all the cakes until they are fully lustred. If you are using the edible varnish, which will add shine to the lustred cake and help the royal iced pearls to adhere, spray the cakes now.

3 Cover the largest cake board (the base board) with black sugar paste, following the technique on page 130. Use a glue stick to attach the black ribbon around the side of the base board. Leave the cakes and board to firm overnight.

4 Trace enough of the template on page 155 to fit around the base tier. Use the scribe to prick the design through onto the base tier first, then reuse the template for the other tiers, working upwards and cutting off the excess paper each time. Omit the middle line of pearls on the top and third tiers, as shown on page 35.

5 Fit the piping bags with the icing nozzles, and fill both bags with black royal icing. Wrap a length of black ribbon around the base of each tier, trim neatly and hold in position with a dab of icing.

6 Pipe the pearl design over the scribed marks, using the no. 2 nozzle for the larger pearls and the no. 1.5 nozzle for the more detailed scalloped design. Leave to firm overnight. Stack the tiers centrally, following the technique on page 141, and dress the top tier with the silk rose.

ASCOT PEARL

Ladies' Day at Royal Ascot is undoubtedly the world's most glamorous race day, when sensational attire and millinery are traditionally worn. This cake was inspired by the black and white Ascot scene in the film of My Fair Lady, starring Audrey Hepburn, whose preferred designer was Hubert de Givenchy.

YOU WILL NEED

15cm (6in), 23cm (9in) and 30cm (12in) round cakes

15cm (6in), 23cm (9in), 30cm (12in) and 38cm (15in) thick round cake boards

marzipan, for the cakes (see page 129 for quantities)

ivory sugar paste, for the cakes (see page 130 for quantities)

black sugar paste, for the base board (see page 131 for quantity)

2.25m (2½ yards) black ribbon with white polka dots 25mm (1in) wide, cut into 50cm (20in), 75cm (30in) and 1m (39in) lengths

sharp scissors

1 quantity royal icing (see page 133), coloured with concentrated black edible food colour

12 dowels

glue stick

1.2m (4ft) black ribbon 15mm (⅝in) wide

piping bag

no. 2 icing nozzle

100g (3½oz) black petal paste

11 white 26-gauge wires, cut into 3

icing sugar, for dusting

small rolling pin

2in (5cm) camellia cutter

white floristry tape

1 Place the cakes on thick cake boards of the same size and cover with marzipan and ivory sugar paste, following the techniques on pages 128 and 130–1. Cover the largest cake board (the base board) with black sugar paste, following the technique on page 130. Leave the cakes and board to firm overnight.

2 Wrap a length of polka-dot ribbon around the base of each tier, trim neatly and hold in position with a dab of royal icing. Stack the tiers centrally, following the techniqe on page 141. Use a glue stick to attach the black ribbon around the edge of the base board.

3 Fit the piping bag with the icing nozzle and fill with black royal icing. Pipe a row of black pearls above each ribbon.

4 To make the camellia, knead the black petal paste until smooth and pliable. Mould a hazelnut-sized piece of petal paste into a square-based cone, 1cm (⅜in) wide x 2cm (¾in) long, and insert a wire at the base.

5 On a clean work surface lightly dusted with icing sugar, roll out the remaining paste to a depth of 3mm (⅛in). Cut out 10 camellia petals, using the cutter, and insert a wire in the base of each. Drape over a cardboard tube covered with cling film to firm overnight.

6 To assemble the camellia, wire 4 petals equidistantly around the central cone, using the white floristry tape to hold them in position as you work.

7 Wire the remaining 6 petals equidistantly behind the first row. Trim the wires at the back of the camellia and set in position.

PEARL FEATHERS

This cake was inspired by the Tiller Girls dancing troupe from the turn of the 20th century, with their glittering costumes of sequins and pearls and ostrich plumes. Delicate white feathers are painted onto a pearl-lustred steel-blue cake, then defined with white pearls. A single orchid provides a feathery 'headdress'.

YOU WILL NEED

10cm (4in), 15cm (6in), 20cm (8in) and 25cm (10in) round cakes

10cm (4in), 15cm (6in), 20cm (8in) and 25cm (10in) thick round cake boards

marzipan, for the cakes (see page 129 for quantities)

steel-blue sugar paste, for the cakes (see page 130 for quantities)

30g (1oz) pearl lustre

18 dowels

scribe

10g (¼oz) cocoa butter

10g (¼oz) white powder dust

small paintbrush

2.3m (2½ yards) white ribbon 9mm (⅜in) wide, cut into 35cm (14in), 50cm (20in), 65cm (26in) and 80cm (32in) lengths

sharp scissors

1 quantity royal icing (see page 133)

piping bag and no. 2 icing nozzle

Cattleya orchid

1 Place the cakes on thick cake boards of the same size and cover with marzipan and steel-blue sugar paste, following the techniques on pages 128 and 130–1. Using your hands, gently rub pearl lustre over each tier. Leave the cakes to firm overnight.

2 Stack the tiers centrally, following the technique on page 141. Use the scribe to mark out the layout of the feathers down over the sides of the entire cake.

3 Melt the cocoa butter by placing it on a saucer over a bowl of freshly boiled water. Add the white powder dust and blend together, then paint the feathers on the cake with this mixture, building up layers and intensity as you work. Leave to dry. Wrap a length of ribbon around the base of each tier, trim neatly and hold in position with a dab of royal icing.

4 Fit the piping bag with the icing nozzle and fill with royal icing. Pipe little pearls over all the main veins of the feathers, then leave to set overnight. Finally, place the orchid on top.

BOWS AND BROOCHES

This timeless and classic cake was inspired by sleek couture bridal gowns with soft pearl-lustre sashes and a detailed bow. You can easily adapt it to suit any wedding theme simply by changing the colour of the icing 'ribbons'. With no floral or other embellishments, all the elements of this elegantly simple cake are edible.

YOU WILL NEED

10cm (4in), 15cm (6in), 20cm (8in) and 25cm (10in) square cakes

10cm (4in), 15cm (6in), 20cm (8in), 25cm (10in) and 33cm (13in) thick square cake boards

marzipan, for the cakes
(see page 129 for quantities)

sugar paste, for the cakes and base board
(see pages 130 and 131 for quantities), plus 1.5kg
(3lb 5oz) for the ribbons, bow and brooch

18 dowels

glue stick

1.5m (5ft) ivory ribbon 15mm (⅝in) wide

icing sugar, for dusting

rolling pin

ruler

sharp knife

flat paintbrush

5cm (2in) and 7.5cm (3in) round cutters

piping bag

no. 1.5 icing nozzle

1 quantity royal icing (see page 133)

45 x 5mm (¼in) silver dragees

10g (¼oz) topaz lustre

2 tsp alcohol dipping solution

1 Place the cakes on thick cake boards of the same size and cover with marzipan and sugar paste, following the techniques on pages 128 and 130–1. Cover the largest cake board (the base board) with sugar paste, following the technique on page 130. Leave the cakes and board to firm overnight.

2 Stack the tiers centrally, following the technique on page 141. Use a glue stick to attach the ivory ribbon around the side of the base board.

3 On a clean work surface lightly dusted with icing sugar, knead the sugar paste for the ribbons, bow and brooch until soft and pliable, then divide into 3. Form one-third into a sausage shape and roll until it is about 1m (39in) long and 3mm (⅛in) thick. Place a ruler gently on the icing and cut along the 2 long edges with a sharp knife; slide the ruler along and cut again, repeating until you have cut a 1m (39in) ribbon of the width of the ruler.

4 Paint around the bottom of the base tier with a little cooled boiled water and carefully wrap the icing ribbon around it, ensuring the base touches the board. Use the knife to trim any excess and join the clean edges together neatly.

5 Roll out another one-third of the paste, adding in the trimmings from the first ribbon, and use it to make ribbons for the other 3 tiers, and also the tails, one 15cm (6in) long and one 18cm (7in) long. Attach the ribbons as before and set the tails aside.

6 To make the bow, roll out a 7.5cm (3in) ball of sugar paste to a depth of 3mm (⅛in) and cut out 2 x 7.5cm (3in) circles. Run a rolling pin over these circles to elongate them slightly, then fold them in half to form 2 loops, joining the shortest sections together. Seal with a little water and set aside.

7 To make the brooch, roll out the remaining sugar paste to a depth of 5mm (¼in) and cut out a 5cm (2in) circle. Fit the piping bag with the icing nozzle and fill with royal icing. Pipe 2 rings of pearls around the outer edge of the brooch and fix the silver dragees into position.

8 Fill in the centre of the brooch with more pearls. Using some royal icing, fix the 2 ribbon tails and bow loops into position on the second tier. Hold the bow in position with cocktail sticks and leave to firm for 4 hours or overnight.

9 Dissolve the topaz lustre in the alcohol dipping solution and brush 2 coats onto all the iced ribbons, the bow and its tails, ensuring all the sides and edges are evenly covered. Lustre the centre of the brooch and finally fix it into position with some royal icing.

CASCADING CRYSTAL ROSE

These roses and lilies cascade down over one side of the cake in much the same way as a luxurious Grecian-style evening gown with a single shoulder strap of corsage blooms by Ben de Lisi. Swarovski crystals dotted among the flowers add sparkle and even more glamour.

YOU WILL NEED

15cm (6in), 20cm (8in) and 25cm (10in) round cakes

15cm (6in), 20cm (8in), 25cm (10in), 33cm (13in) and 40cm (16in) thick round cake boards

marzipan, for the cakes (see page 129 for quantities)

sugar paste, for the cakes (see page 130 for quantities), plus 300g (10½oz) for the roses

black sugar paste, for the base boards (see page 131 for quantities)

4.35m (4¾ yards) black double satin ribbon 15mm (⅝in) wide, cut into 1.1m (44in) and 1.3m (52in) lengths for the base boards and 50cm (20in), 65cm (26in) and 80cm (32in) lengths for the cakes

glue stick

1 quantity royal icing (see page 133), coloured with concentrated black edible food colour, for the pearls, plus extra white icing to fix the flowers

12 dowels

scribe

ruler

sharp scissors

1.95m (2⅛ yards) silver ribbon 9mm (⅜in) wide, cut into 50cm (20in), 65cm (26in) and 80cm (32in) lengths

piping bag

no. 3 icing nozzle

150 silver dragees

12 white sugar lilies (see page 144)

5 white 28-gauge wires, cut into 3

15 Swarovski 10mm (⅜in) bicone crystal beads

1 Place the cakes on thick cake boards of the same size and cover with marzipan and sugar paste, following the techniques on pages 128 and 130–1. Cover the 2 largest boards (the base boards) with black sugar paste, following the technique on page 130. Make 15 hand-moulded roses, following the technique on page 136. Leave the cakes, boards and roses to firm overnight.

2 Fix black ribbon around the edge of the base boards using a glue stick. Stack the boards together, using icing to fix them. Stack the tiers centrally, following the technique on page 141 and place on the stacked boards.

3 Scribe a line around the base of each tier using a ruler width as a gauge. Wrap black ribbon around the base of each tier, trim neatly and hold in place with a dab of royal icing. Repeat with silver ribbon, aligned at each tier base.

4 Fit the piping bag with the icing nozzle and fill with black royal icing. Pipe a row of black pearl drops around each tier, finishing at the scribed line.

5 Pipe a single pearl at the top of each pearl drop and place a silver dragee in position. Leave to set. Fix a cascade of roses and lilies from the top tier down over one side of the cake with white icing. Push a wire length through one of the crystals until the crystal is halfway along the wire. Bend the wire over so that the halves meet under the crystal and twist to secure. Repeat with the other crystals and wires. Push the Swarovski crystals in between the roses and the lilies to finish.

country rose

ANTIQUE ROSE

This cake uses the more traditional royal icing, rather than sugar paste. It is decorated with piped scrolls and pearls, finished with tiny handmade rosebuds and blocked with fresh flowers. It is formal yet romantic and elegant, dressed with muted colours of dusky pink, lime green and antique ivory.

YOU WILL NEED

15cm (6in), 23cm (9in) and 30cm (12in) square cakes

23cm (9in), 30cm (12in) and 38cm (15in) thick square cake boards

marzipan, for the cakes
(see page 129 for quantities)

royal icing (see page 133), coloured with concentrated ivory edible food colour, for the cakes (see page 134 for quantities), plus 300g (10½oz) for the boards and 1 quantity for the piping

100g (3½oz) dusky pink petal paste

100g (3½oz) lime green petal paste

icing sugar, for dusting

small rolling pin

small knife

tracing paper and pen

scribe

piping bag

no. 2 icing nozzle

3.6m (12ft) ivory ribbon 15mm (⅝in) wide, cut into 90cm (36in), 1.2m (48in) and 1.5m (60in) lengths

glue stick

10 dowels

12cm (5in) and 20cm (8in) polystyrene blocks 5cm (2in) deep

floristry wires, cut into 3

Cymbidium orchids, Vandella roses and guelder rose

1 Place the cakes on their base boards and cover with marzipan and ivory royal icing, following the techniques on page 129 and 134. Leave the cakes to firm overnight.

2 To make the rosebuds, knead both petal pastes until soft and pliable. On a clean work surface lightly dusted with icing sugar, roll out the pastes very thinly – roughly 1mm (¹⁄₁₆in) – and cut into 1cm (⅜in) wide strips.

3 Roll up one of the paste strips to create a small rosebud. Trim and repeat until you have 72 rosebuds in each colour.

4 Trace the design from the template on page 155 and scribe it onto the side of each tier.

5 Fit the piping bag with the icing nozzle and fill with ivory royal icing. Pipe a trail of pearls around the base of each tier, then pipe the scribed design onto the sides. Use royal icing to fix the rosebuds, in pairs of each colour, in place. Fix a length of ribbon around the edge of each base board using a glue stick.

6 Block the tiers with the flowers, following the technique on page 140. Dress the top tier to finish.

VINTAGE ROSE CROWN

Many bridal gowns make good use of vintage lace and covered buttons. I was inspired by the Spanish designer Rosa Clara for this design, with topaz-lustred detail on a four-tier stacked ivory wedding cake. I have crowned this cake with a vintage-style tiara and delicately scented garden roses.

YOU WILL NEED

15cm (6in), 20cm (8in), 25cm (10in) and 30cm (12in) round cakes

15cm (6in), 20cm (8in), 25cm (10in), 30cm (12in) and 38cm (15in) thick round cake boards

marzipan, for the cakes (see page 129 for quantities)

ivory sugar paste, for the cakes and base board (see pages 130 and 131 for quantities)

1.2m (4ft) ivory ribbon 15mm (⅝in) wide

glue stick

2.95m (3⅛ yards) ivory ribbon 12mm (⅜in) wide, cut into 50cm (20in), 65cm (26in), 80cm (32in) and 1m (39in) lengths

sharp scissors

1 quantity royal icing (see page 133), coloured with concentrated ivory edible food colour

18 dowels

scribe

2 piping bags

nos. 1.5 and 4 icing nozzles

38cm (15in) diameter cake stand

David Austin scented white garden roses

tiara

1 Place the cakes on cake boards of the same size and cover with marzipan and ivory sugar paste, following the techniques on pages 128 and 130–1. Cover the largest cake board (the base board) with ivory sugar paste, following the technique on page 130. Leave the cakes and board to firm overnight.

2 Fix the length of 15mm (⅝in) ribbon around the edge of the base board using a glue stick. Wrap a length of 12mm (⅜in) ribbon around the base of each tier, trim neatly and hold in position with a dab of royal icing. Stack the tiers, following the technique on page 141.

3 Using the picture opposite, scribe the design onto the second and third tiers to create a scalloped effect. Scribe the outline of the panels on the base tier. Fit the piping bags with the icing nozzles and fill with ivory royal icing. Use the no. 1.5 nozzle to pipe a filigree edge to the design and fill in with cornelli piping (an elaborate lace-like pattern; see detail on page 52). Repeat this technique with the panels on the base tier and edge these with a pearl trail.

4 Use the no. 4 nozzle to pipe a vertical trail of pearl 'buttons' down the centre of the design.

5 Pipe delicate pearls above the ribbon edge at regular 1cm (½in) intervals on every tier.

6 Place the cake on the cake stand, position a dome of fresh roses on the top tier and set the tiara in front to hold the roses in position.

LACE VEIL

Lace veils create an ethereal entrance to a wedding. Jasper Conran uses the most delicate of lace in his designs, and I have hand-brushed my own piped lace design on this cake for similar effect. The cake was lustred and stacked offset before the lace veil was iced in place. Fresh roses complete the picture.

YOU WILL NEED

15cm (6in), 23cm (9in) and 30cm (12in) round cakes

15cm (6in), 23cm (9in) and 30cm (12in) thick round cake boards

marzipan, for the cakes
(see page 129 for quantities)

caramel sugar paste, for the cakes
(see page 130 for quantities)

30g (1oz) topaz lustre

12 dowels

tracing paper and pen

scribe

2.25m (2½ yards) ivory ribbon 15mm (⅝in) wide, cut into 50cm (20in), 75cm (30in) and 1m (39in) lengths

sharp scissors

1 quantity royal icing (see page 133), coloured with concentrated ivory edible food colour

2 piping bags

nos. 1.5 and 2 icing nozzles

3 dusky pink roses

1 Place the cakes on thick cake boards of the same size and cover with marzipan and caramel sugar paste, following the techniques on pages 128 and 130–1. Rub the topaz lustre over the top and sides of all the tiers. Leave the cakes to firm overnight.

2 Stack the tiers, following the technique on page 141, but offset towards the back rather than placed centrally.

3 Trace the design from the template on page 152 and scribe the scalloped outline edge to the lace veil, starting on the top tier and trailing down over the 3 tiers. Wrap a length of ribbon around the base of each tier, trim neatly and hold in position with a dab of ivory royal icing.

4 Fit the piping bags with the nozzles and fill with icing. Use the no. 2 nozzle to pipe the flower lace design within the scribed veil outline.

5 Dip a fine paintbrush in water and brush the edges of the design inwards to create an embroidery effect. Continue to pipe all the detail within the veil area, then use the no. 1.5 nozzle to pipe over the scribed lines to mark the outline edge of the veil, with its pearls and fringing (see detail on page 53).

6 Present the cake on a white cake stand and dress with dusky pink roses.

MANDARIN

This cake, covered in white chocolate fans and blocked with flowers, was inspired both by beautiful Victorian fans, which were often made from lace with optional fringe, tassels and marabou feathers, and by their modern-day counterparts of Chinese and Thai paper and bamboo fans.

YOU WILL NEED

15cm (6in), 23cm (9in) and 30cm (12in) round cakes

15cm (6in), 23cm (9in) and 30cm (12in) thick round cake boards

white chocolate plastique (see page 135), for the cakes (see page 129 for quantities), plus 2.1kg (4¾lb) for the roses and leaves and 1.5kg (3¼lb) for the fans

4cm (1¾in) rose-leaf plunger veiner and cutter

icing sugar, for dusting

small rolling pin

sharp knife

pastry brush

100g (3½oz) white chocolate, melted

10cm (4in) and 15cm (6in) polystyrene columns 7.5cm (3in) deep

10 dowels

17 floristry wires, cut into 3

30 roses, 20 cymbidium orchids and 2 bunches of lilac

1 Place the cakes on thick cake boards of the same size and cover with 2 coats of white chocolate plastique, following the techniques for marzipan and sugar paste on pages 128 and 130–1. Leave the cakes to firm overnight.

2 Use the 1.15kg (2lb 8oz) white chocolate plastique to make 30 hand-moulded roses, following the technique on page 136 and using 25g (1oz) plastique per rose, and 40 rose leaves, using the leaf plunger veiner and cutter, following the technique on page 110 and using 10g (¼oz) per leaf.

3 To make the fans, knead the 1.5kg (3¼lb) plastique until soft and pliable. Lightly dust a clean work surface with icing sugar and roll out the plastique to a depth of 5mm (¼in). Using a sharp knife, cut a rectangle approximately 20 x 15cm (8 x 6in) and form it into pleats, working from one of the long sides. Fold the pleated length in half to create a fan and set aside to firm up. Repeat with the remaining rolled-out plastique until you have a total of 30 fans.

4 Using the pastry brush, paint the back of one fan with melted chocolate and fix it to the side of the base tier. Continue around the entire tier, using 12 of the fans, then fill the gaps with roses and leaves. Repeat with the other 2 tiers, using 8 fans for the middle tier and 10 for the top, making sure you cover the top as well as the sides of the top tier.

5 Block the tiers with the flowers, following the technique on page 140. Dress the top tier to finish.

TIP

Allow the fans and roses to come just higher than the top of each cake so the fresh flowers tuck through nicely when the cake is blocked.

CHOCOLATE ROSE POLKA DOT

Polka dots have always been fashionable, youthful and fun. They may be used in a contrasting colour for a more dramatic effect, or tonal as I have chosen for this cake – very much in the style of a jacquard weave. The tiers have been gently raised and the gaps blocked with hand-moulded white chocolate roses.

YOU WILL NEED

15cm (6in), 23cm (9in), 30cm (12in) and 38cm (15in) round cakes

15cm (6in), 23cm (9in), 30cm (12in), 38cm (15in) and 45cm (18in) thick round cake boards

17.25kg (38lb 4oz) white chocolate plastique (see page 135) – 12.95kg (28lb 8oz) for the cakes, 2.2kg (5lb) for the board, 2kg (4lb 8oz) for the roses and 100g (3½oz) for the polka dots

4.9m (5⅓ yards) cream grosgrain ribbon 15mm (⅝in) wide, cut into 50cm (20in), 75cm (30in), 1m (40in), 1.2m (48in) and 1.45m (57in) lengths

glue stick

sharp scissors

royal icing (see page 133), for fixing

icing sugar, for dusting

small rolling pin

2cm (¾in) diameter polka-dot plunger cutter

sugar glue

18 dowels

12cm (5in), 20cm (8in) and 28cm (11in) polystyrene columns 2.5cm (1in) deep

1 Place the cakes on thick cake boards of the same size and cover with a double layer of white chocolate plastique, following the techniques for applying marzipan and sugar paste on pages 128 and 130–1. Cover the largest board (the base board) with white chocolate plastique. Leave the cakes and board to firm overnight.

2 Fix a length of ribbon around the edge of the base board using a glue stick. Also, wrap a length of ribbon around the base of each tier, trim neatly and hold in position with a dab of royal icing.

3 Use the white chocolate plastique to make 50 hand-moulded roses, 7cm (2¾in) in diameter, following the technique on page 136, teasing the petals out to make a thinner, frilled edge. Leave to firm.

4 To make the polka dots, knead the white chocolate plastique until it is soft and pliable. On a clean work surface lightly dusted with icing sugar, roll out the white chocolate plastique to a depth of 2mm (⅛in). Use the polka-dot plunger cutter to stamp out approximately 60 polka dots.

5 Position the polka dots randomly over the cake, using sugar glue to fix them in position.

6 Prepare the cakes for blocking with flowers, following the technique on page 140, but do not add the flowers in step 3. Stack the tiers into position, using some icing on top of each polystyrene column to hold the tier above in position, then add the roses, using icing to hold them in place.

TIP
Royal icing is stronger to hold the tiers and roses in position than melted white chocolate.

YOU WILL NEED

37 x 5cm (2in) square cakes
(see page 132 for cutting instructions)

marzipan, for the cakes
(see page 132 for quantities)

ivory sugar paste, for the cakes and the stand
(see pages 132 and 131 for quantities)

20cm (8in), 25cm (10in) and 30cm (12in) thick
square cake boards

6m (6½ yards) ivory ribbon 15mm (⅝in) wide, cut into
80cm (32in), 1m (39in) and 1.2m (48in) lengths
for the boards; the rest for the blocks

10cm (4in) and 15cm (6in) polystyrene blocks 7.5cm (3in) deep

piping bag

royal icing (see page 133), coloured with
concentrated ivory edible food colour, for fixing

sharp scissors

4m (4½ yards) dusky pink organza ribbon
15mm (⅝in) wide, cut into 20cm (8in) lengths

4m (4½ yards) brown organza ribbon
15mm (⅝in) wide, cut into 20cm (8in) lengths

40 sugar rosebuds with green calyxes
(see page 145) – 20 dusky pink, 20 brown

ROSEBUDS *These delicate individual parcel cakes have been topped with a single rosebud and tied with an organza ribbon in a complementing colour. They are perfect for a more intimate wedding or civil partnership and can be served one per guest with Champagne or coffee. Alternatively, they could be taken home as mementoes.*

1 Cover the cakes with marzipan and ivory sugar paste, following the techniques on page 132. Prepare a 3-tier iced stand using the cake boards, sugar paste, ivory ribbon and polystyrene blocks listed, following the technique on page 139 to the end of step 4. Leave the cakes and stand to firm overnight.

2 Fill a piping bag with ivory royal icing and snip the end with sharp scissors. Pipe a pearl in the centre of each cake and place a rosebud in position.

3 Wrap a length of organza ribbon around the middle of each cake, matching the rosebud colour, and secure with a double knot. Trim the ends with the sharp scissors.

4 Place the cakes on each tier of the stand, alternating colours, with all the ribbon ties facing outwards. Assemble the stand following step 5 on page 139.

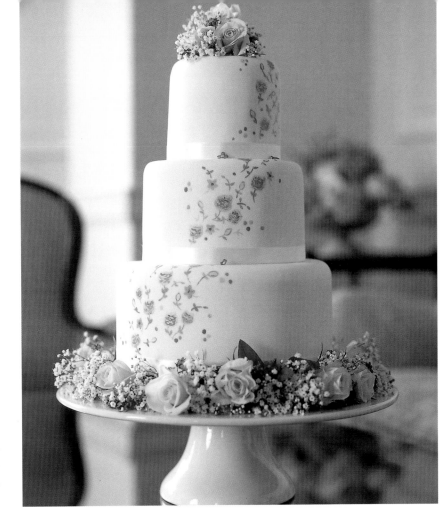

10cm (4in), 15cm (6in) and 20cm (8in) round cakes

10cm (4in), 15cm (6in) and 20cm (8in) thick round cake boards

marzipan, for the cakes (see page 129 for quantities)

sugar paste, for the cakes (see page 130 for quantities)

1.5m (1⅝ yards) white ribbon 15mm (⅝in) wide, cut into 35cm (14in), 50cm (20in) and 65cm (26in) lengths

sharp scissors

royal icing (see page 133), coloured with concentrated ivory edible food colour, for fixing

12 dowels

25g (1oz) cocoa butter

powder dusts in pinks, greens, blues and white

fine paintbrushes

12 pale pink rosebuds, gypsophilia and forget-me-nots

15cm (6in) polystyrene column 5cm (2in) deep

38cm (15in) diameter cake stand

PETITE ROSE

The hand-painted roses and buds on this smaller, three-tier cake can be repeated on several individual cakes for presentation to the bridesmaids or flower girls as mementoes. Beautifully intricate and individual, this cake does not follow a strict template, so the finished result will be expressive and completely unique.

1 Place the cakes on thick cake boards of the same size and cover with marzipan and sugar paste, following the techniques on pages 128 and 130–1. Leave the cakes to firm overnight.

2 Wrap a length of ribbon around the base of each tier, trim neatly and hold in position with a dab of royal icing. Stack the cakes following the technique on page 141.

3 Melt the cocoa butter by placing it on a saucer over a bowl of freshly boiled water. Place the powder dusts in a palette and blend a little cocoa butter with each one as needed. (If the cocoa butter begins to harden during the painting process, place the saucer over more freshly boiled water.) Using the design template on page 151 as a guide, paint roses and buds on the top tier and cascading down over the cake to the opposite side at the base. Using shades of pink, blue and green, fill in with stalks, leaves, tiny blue forget-me-not flowers and spots. Leave to dry. Wire the roses, following the technique on page 145.

4 Place the polystyrene column on the cake stand and stud with the fresh flowers. Place the stacked cake on top and dress the top tier with a small arrangement of similar fresh flowers.

fun and funky

RAINBOW DROPS

Cute and colourful, these individual cakes are stylish yet funky. Hand piped with bright drops of coloured royal icing concentrating towards the base of each tier like Champagne bubbles, they look fabulous en masse set on a stand and served with chilled pink Champagne.

YOU WILL NEED

33 x 5cm (2in) round cakes
(see page 132 for cutting instructions)

10cm (4in) round cake

10cm (4in) thin round cake board

marzipan, for all the cakes
(see pages 129 and 132 for quantities)

ivory sugar paste, for all the cakes and the stand
(see pages 130, 132 and 139 for quantities)

18cm (7in), 23cm (9in), 28cm (11in) and 33cm
(13in) thick round cake boards

3.3m (3⅔ yards) orange ribbon 15mm (⅝in) wide,
cut into 55cm (22in), 75cm (30in), 90cm (36in)
and 110cm (44in) lengths

7m (7⅔ yards) white ribbon 15mm (⅝in) wide

10cm (4in), 12cm (5in) and 15cm (6in)
polystyrene columns 7.5cm (3in) deep

3 piping bags

3 x no. 1.5 icing nozzles

1 quantity royal icing (see page 133),
divided into 3 and coloured with concentrated
edible food colours as follows: ⅓ fuchsia pink,
⅓ orange and ⅓ leaf green

6.95m (7½ yards) green ribbon 9mm (⅜in) wide,
cut into 20cm (8in) lengths

sharp scissors

1 Cover all the cakes with marzipan and ivory sugar paste, following the techniques on pages 128, 130–1 and 132, and putting the large cake on a thin board first. Prepare a 4-tier iced stand, using the cake boards, sugar paste, orange and white ribbons and polystyrene columns listed left, following the technique on page 139 to the end of step 4. Leave the cakes and stand to firm overnight.

2 Fit the piping bags with the icing nozzles and fill each with one colour of royal icing. Wrap a length of green ribbon around the base of each cake, trim neatly and hold in position with a dab of icing. Pipe tiny pearls on each cake, concentrating them towards the base of each cake and letting them peter out towards the top.

3 Place the little cakes on the lower 3 tiers of the stand, with all the ribbon joins facing inwards. Assemble the stand following step 5 on page 139 and place the 10cm (4in) cake on the top tier.

COUTURE CONFETTI

One of my favourite parts of a wedding is confetti being liberally thrown over the happy couple. I thought it would be fun to create a wedding cake with delicate piped confetti (horseshoes, hearts and a picot triangle of pearls joined together) photographed with fresh rose petals showering down over it. Et voila!

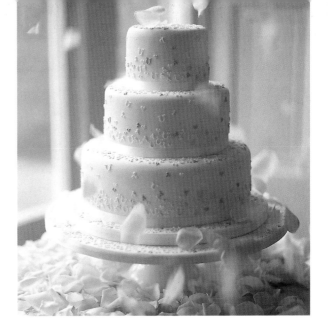

YOU WILL NEED

15cm (6in), 23cm (9in) and 30cm (12in) round cakes

15cm (6in), 23cm (9in), 30cm (12in), 38cm (15in) and 45cm (18in) thick round cake boards

marzipan, for the cakes (see page 129 for quantities)

sugar paste, for the cakes and 2 base boards (see pages 130 and 131 for quantities)

4.9m (5⅓ yards) white ribbon 15mm (⅝in) wide, cut into 50cm (20in), 75cm (30in) and 1m (39in) lengths for the cakes and 1.2m (48in) and 1.45m (57in) lengths for the base boards

sharp scissors

1 quantity royal icing (see page 133), divided into 4 and coloured with concentrated edible food colours as follows: ¼ ivory, ¼ pink, ¼ fuchsia and ¼ left white

glue stick

12 dowels

4 piping bags

4 x no. 1.5 icing nozzles

1 Place the cakes on thick cake boards of the same size and cover with marzipan and sugar paste, following the techniques on pages 128 and 130–1. Cover the 2 largest boards (the base boards) with sugar paste, following the technique on page 130. Leave the cakes and boards to firm overnight.

2 Wrap a length of ribbon around the base of each tier, trim neatly and hold in position with a dab of royal icing. Fix a length of ribbon around the base boards using a glue stick and fix the boards together with a dab of royal icing. Stack the tiers centrally on the stacked base boards, following the technique on page 141.

3 Fit the piping bags with icing nozzles and fill each with a different coloured royal icing. Using the template design on page 152 as a guide only, pipe 'falling' confetti on the top and sides of each tier. Ensure the top of each tier and the base boards are well covered with confetti, as they would be if it had freshly fallen, but concentrate the design around the base of the sides of the tiers, petering out towards the top of the sides of the tiers.

TIP

I found it easier to pipe this design working with one colour at a time — going all over and around each tier before moving on with the next colour.

RUFFLE TRUFFLE

This chocolate sculptural creation oozes rich, indulgent decadence. The cake (preferably the chocolate truffle torte on page 146) is topped with a cone wrapped around with dark chocolate plastique ruffles, filled with chocolate frills brushed with gold leaf. This cake has been heavily glazed and would complement a Versace-inspired wedding.

YOU WILL NEED

30cm (12in) round cake

30cm (12in) thin round cake board

white chocolate plastique (see page 135), for the cake (see page 129 for quantity)

dark chocolate plastique (see page 136), for the cake and base board (see pages 129 and 131 for quantities, and Tip below), plus 3 quantities for the ruffles, ribbon and bow

475g (1lb 1oz) sugar paste

40cm (16in) thick round cake board

500g (1lb 2oz) plain chocolate, melted

6 dowels

glue stick

25cm (10in) polystyrene cone 45cm (18in) high

25cm (10in) thin round cake board

7.5cm (3in) flat paintbrush

large and small rolling pins

cocoa powder, for dusting

sharp knife

2.5cm (1in) flat paintbrush

20 x 15cm (6in) squares of gold leaf

edible spray varnish

1.3m (52in) dark brown grosgrain ribbon 15mm (⅝in) wide

1 Place the cake on the thin cake board and cover with a first coat of white chocolate plastique and a second coat of dark chocolate plastique mixed 1:1 with sugar paste, following the techniques for marzipan and sugar paste on pages 128 and 130–1. Cover the thick board (the base board) with dark chocolate plastique, following the technique for sugar paste on page 130. Leave the cake and board to firm overnight.

2 Fix the cake in position on the base board with a little melted chocolate. Dowel the cake to the top of the tier, following the technique on page 141. Use a glue stick to fix the polystyrene cone to the 25cm (10in) thin board. Paint a little melted chocolate on the top of the cake with the 7.5cm (3in) paintbrush and fix the cone in position.

3 Set aside 200g (7oz) of the 3 quantities of dark chocolate plastique and knead the remainder until smooth and pliable. In sections, roll out a strip 15cm (6in) wide and 3mm (⅛in) thick on a work surface lightly dusted with cocoa powder. Trim one long edge with a sharp knife and 'feather' the other long edge by rolling it with a small rolling pin until it starts to wave.

4 Use the 7.5cm (3in) paintbrush to brush the bottom of the cone and the sides of the cake with melted chocolate.

5 Starting at the base of the cake and working before the chocolate dries, wrap the length of chocolate collar around the cake, ensuring the clean, sharp edge is flush with the base board. Wrap it right around the base, then start working upwards, painting more of the cone as you go, rolling out and adding more chocolate plastique collars until you reach the top of the cake, where you should finish with a flourish.

6 Roll out smaller strips of chocolate plastique 5cm (2in) wide x 3mm (⅛in) thick and fold them up to create frills. Fix these in position inside the ruffles.

7 Use the 2.5cm (1in) paintbrush to lift gold off the gold leaf sheets and dust it on the edge of the frills.

8 To make the ribbon and bow, knead the set-aside dark chocolate plastique until smooth and pliable. On a clean work surface lightly dusted with cocoa powder, roll out the plastique into a 3mm (⅛in) thick long strip and cut out a piece 1.5m x 6cm (5ft x 2½in). Cut off a 30cm (12in) length for the bow. Fix the long ribbon remaining around the base of the cake and hold it in position with melted chocolate. Cut the 30cm (12in) strip into a 20cm (8in) and a 10cm (4in) length. Fold the 20cm (8in) strip in half and fix this at the front of the cake, opening up the 2 sides of the bow. Finish with the 10cm (4in) strip positioned vertically as the central element of the bow. Trim with a sharp knife to fit.

9 Spray all over with the varnish – lightly for a sheen or heavily for a high shine – and fix the piece of grosgrain ribbon around the edge of the base board using a glue stick.

TIP

The dark chocolate plastique layer is mixed 1:1 with sugar paste, so halve the quantity of plastique given in the chart on page 129.

FLAMENCO

As the name implies, this cake was inspired by the seductive Spanish senoritas in their black and white polka-dot flamenco dresses, clicking their castanets. I have created this dramatic design with a black frill over one side of the entire cake, which has been varnished with black glitter and dressed with red roses.

YOU WILL NEED

15cm (6in), 20cm (8in) and 25cm (10in) round cakes

15cm (6in), 20cm (8in), 25cm (10in) and
35cm (14in) thick round cake boards

marzipan, for the cakes
(see page 129 for quantities)

black sugar paste, for the cakes and base board
(see pages 130 and 131 for quantities)

3.05m (3⅓ yards) black ribbon 15mm (⅝in) wide,
cut into 50cm (20in), 65cm (26in), 80cm (32in) and
1.15m (45in) lengths

sharp scissors

royal icing (see page 133). for fixing

glue stick

12 dowels

scribe

200g (7oz) black petal paste

icing sugar, for dusting

small rolling pin

7.5cm (3in) diameter frill cutter

frilling tool

small knife

2cm (¾in) flat paintbrush

edible spray varnish

15g (½oz) edible black glitter

75g (2½oz) sugar paste

polka-dot plunger cutter

sugar glue

1.5m (5ft) black organza ribbon
35mm (1½in) wide

3.5cm (1½in) decorative button

3 Red Ecstasy roses

1 Place the cakes on thick cake boards of the same size and cover with marzipan and black sugar paste, following the techniques on pages 128 and 130–1. Cover the largest cake board (the base board) with black sugar paste. Leave the cakes and board to firm overnight.

2 Wrap a length of 15mm (⅝in) ribbon around the base of each tier, trim neatly and hold in position with a dab of royal icing. Fix a length of the same ribbon around the edge of the base board using a glue stick. Stack the tiers centrally on the base board, following the technique on page 141. Scribe an inverted V from the top to the bottom of the tiers, measuring around 20cm (8in) at the base.

3 Knead one walnut-sized ball at a time of the black petal paste until soft and pliable. Lightly dust a clean work surface with icing sugar and roll the paste out to a depth of 2.5mm (⅛in). Stamp out the frill and its centre with the frill cutter.

4 Use the frilling tool to thin and frill the outer edge of the frill. Cut the frill right through at one section so that it opens out into a strip.

5 Starting at the base of the cake, use the paintbrush horizontally to dampen the cake with water between the 2 scribed marks, 2–3cm (around 1in) from the base of the tier. Line up one edge of the frill with the scribed inverted V, with the flat section of the frill uppermost and flush with the cake, frilly side pointing towards the base and frilling away from the cake. Trim the frill to fit flush within the inverted V.

6 Make more frills one at a time to prevent the paste drying out, and lay on top of the previous one so that the flat flush parts are covered by the frilly part of the frill above. Repeat until the entire inverted V is filled with frills. Spray the frills with varnish and sprinkle with glitter.

7 Knead the plain sugar paste until soft and pliable. Lightly dust a clean work surface with icing sugar and roll out the paste to a depth of 2.5mm (⅛in). Use the polka-dot plunger cutter to stamp out white circles 2cm (¾in) in diameter and fix these randomly over the entire cake with sugar glue.

8 To make the organza bow, thread 1m (39in) of the ribbon through the back of the decorative button. Tie the ribbon in a double bow and trim the tails with sharp scissors. Fix this ribbon and bow in position with royal icing at the top of the frill. Tie the roses with the remaining length of ribbon and arrange on the top tier.

TIP

The frill is constructed from rows of separate frills adhered to the cake to create one large frill. Petal paste dries out very quickly, so it is essential that you work on just one row of the frill at a time. Keep the remaining petal paste in a sealed polythene bag while you are working.

CHOCOLATE PLEATS

This beautifully structured cake features pleats of white chocolate blocked with fresh green flowers. Vera Wang and the Lebanese designer Elie Saab create feminine, voluminous gowns with material folds and pleats, which would complement this cake perfectly.

YOU WILL NEED

10cm (4in), 15cm (6in), 20cm (8in) and 25cm (10in) square cakes

10cm (4in), 15cm (6in), 20cm (8in), 25cm (10in) and 33cm (13in) thick square cake boards

white chocolate plastique (see page 135), for the cakes and the board (see pages 129 and 131 for quantities), plus 2 quantities to make the pleats

1.3m (52in) cream grosgrain ribbon 15mm (⅝in) wide

glue stick

100g (3½oz) white chocolate, melted

icing sugar, for dusting

rolling pin

ruler

sharp knife

piping bag

12 dowels

7.5cm (3in), 10cm (4in) and 12cm (5in) square polystyrene blocks 2.5cm (1in) deep

floristry wires, cut into 3

guelder rose, green hydrangea, green chrysanthemums and chrysanthemum pom poms

1 Place the cakes on thick cake boards of the same size and cover with white chocolate plastique, following the technique for marzipan on page 128. Cover the largest cake board (the base board) with white chocolate plastique, following the technique shown for sugar paste on page 130. Leave the cakes and board to firm overnight.

2 Fix the length of ribbon around the edge of the base board using a glue stick. Place the base tier centrally on the base board, fixing it in place with a little melted white chocolate. Knead the remaining white chocolate plastique until smooth and pliable. Dust a clean work surface lightly with icing sugar and roll out the white chocolate plastique to a depth of 2mm (⅛in). Use a ruler to cut strips measuring 4 x 10cm (1¼ x 4in). Leave to firm. Repeat to give a total of approximately 125 strips.

3 Fill the piping bag with melted chocolate. Starting with the base tier, pipe a line vertically on the cake and position a pleat in place. Repeat with the next pleat, overlapping the first, and continue until the entire tier is covered with pleats. Repeat with the other tiers. Leave to set.

4 Block the tiers with the flowers, following the technique on page 140. Dress the top tier to finish.

GLITTER RAINBOW ROSES *These vibrant-coloured cakes, topped with glitter-encrusted roses, were inspired by John Galliano, who can always be relied on to use bold, bright, vivid colours. Presenting these daring cakes at an all-white wedding ensures they will certainly take centre stage.*

YOU WILL NEED

77 x 5cm (2in) round cakes
(see page 132 for cutting instructions)

marzipan, for the cakes (see page 132 for quantities)

red, orange, yellow, green, blue and purple sugar paste, for the cakes (see page 132 for quantities); for the stand (see page 131 for quantities); plus the following quantities for the roses: 140g (5oz) red, 180g (6oz) orange, 240g (8½oz) yellow, 300g (10½oz) green, 340g (12oz) blue and 400g (14oz) purple

20cm (8in), 25cm (10in), 30cm (12in), 35cm (14in), 40cm (16in) and 45cm (18in) thick round cake boards

lengths of coloured 15mm (⅝in) ribbon for the stand as follows: 1.6m (1¾ yards) red; 2m (2⅛ yards) orange; 2.4m (2⅔ yards) yellow; 2.6m (3 yards) green; 3m (3¼ yards) blue and 3.4m (3¾ yards) purple

glue stick

10cm (4in), 12cm (5in), 15cm (6in), 18cm (7in) and 20cm (8in) polystyrene columns 7.5cm (3in) deep

paintbrush

sugar glue

red, orange, yellow, green, blue and purple edible glitter

piping bag

1 quantity royal icing (see page 133)

sharp scissors

lengths of coloured 15mm (⅝in) ribbon for the cakes as follows: 1.85m (2 yards) red; 2.6m (3 yards) orange; 3.4m (3¾ yards) yellow; 3.95m (4¼ yards) green; 4.5m (5 yards) blue and 5.45m (6 yards) purple

1 Cover the cakes with marzipan and sugar paste, following the techniques on page 132. Make 7 red cakes, 9 orange, 12 yellow, 15 green, 17 blue and 20 purple. Prepare a 6-tier iced stand using the cake boards, coloured sugar pastes, coloured ribbons and polystyrene columns listed left, following the technique on page 139 to the end of step 4. Leave the cakes and stand to firm overnight.

2 Make the same number of hand-moulded roses as there are cakes, using the different-coloured sugar pastes and following the technique on page 136. Leave to firm, then brush the top of each rose liberally with sugar glue.

3 Working from little dishes of each of the different coloured glitters, sprinkle some same-colour glitter over each rose until it is fully encrusted. Upturn each rose to remove the excess glitter.

4 Fill the piping bag with royal icing and snip the end with sharp scissors. Pipe a pearl in the centre of each individual cake and place the rose in position.

5 Wrap a length of same-colour ribbon around the base of each cake, trim neatly and hold in position with a dab of icing.

6 Place the cakes on the tiers of the stand with all the ribbon joins facing inwards. Assemble the stand following step 5 on page 139.

creative

PEARLIQUE

This design is so simple, yet so effective and is undoubtedly one of my favourites. I was inspired to design a cake that was delicate and feminine and felt fresh and innocent. I have chosen to present this cake with a barefoot charm — no base board, no flowers, no cake stand, just a beautiful bridal bouquet.

YOU WILL NEED

10cm (4in), 15cm (6in), 20cm (8in) and 25cm (10in) square cakes

10cm (4in), 15cm (6in), 20cm (8in) and 25cm (10in) thick square cake boards

marzipan, for the cakes (see page 129 for quantities)

sugar paste, for the cakes (see page 130 for quantities)

2.8m (3 yards) white ribbon 15mm (⅝in) wide, cut into 40cm (16in), 60cm (24in), 80cm (32in) and 1m (39in) lengths

sharp scissors

2 quantities royal icing (see page 133)

2 piping bags

nos. 1.5 and 2 icing nozzles

18 dowels

1 Place the cakes on thick cake boards of the same size and cover with marzipan and sugar paste, following the techniques on pages 128 and 130–1. Leave the cakes to firm overnight.

2 Wrap a length of ribbon around the base of each tier, trim neatly and hold in position with a dab of royal icing. Fit the piping bags with the icing nozzles and fill with royal icing. Use the no. 1.5 nozzle to pipe a row of tiny pearls 1cm (⅜in) apart just above the ribbon, then pipe a grid of 1cm (⅜in) long straight lines randomly over the sides and top of the cakes.

3 Use the no. 2 nozzle to pipe pearls randomly over the lines to encrust the tiers (see detail on page 80). Leave to set for 4 hours or overnight.

4 Stack the tiers centrally, following the technique on page 141.

EASTERN PROMISE

I was inspired by a stunning embroidered and beaded tailored jacket for this cake. The design comprises a lotus flower, regarded as a symbol of divine beauty by Hindus, which is painted on, and then each flower is outlined with piped icing and interspersed with pearls. The entire design is then lustred with gold.

YOU WILL NEED

15cm (6in), 20cm (8in) and 25cm (10in) hexagonal cakes

15cm (6in), 20cm (8in), 25cm (10in) and 33cm (13in) thick hexagonal cake boards

marzipan, for the cakes (see page 129 for quantities)

ivory sugar paste, for the cakes and base board (see pages 130 and 131 for quantities)

3.7m (4 yards) gold ribbon 15mm (⅝in) wide, cut into 60cm (24in), 80cm (32in), 1m (39in) and 1.3m (52in) lengths

sharp scissors

1 quantity royal icing (see page 133), coloured with concentrated old gold edible food colour

glue stick

12 dowels

25g (1oz) cocoa butter

10g (¼oz) turquoise powder dust

fine paintbrush

piping bag

no 1.5 icing nozzle

2 tsp gold lustre

1 tbsp alcohol dipping solution

1 Place the cakes on thick cake boards of the same size and cover with marzipan and ivory sugar paste, following the techniques on pages 128 and 130–1. Cover the largest board (the base board) with sugar paste, following the technique on page 130. Leave the cakes and board to firm overnight.

2 Wrap a length of ribbon around the base of each tier, trim neatly and hold in position with a dab of royal icing. Fix the remaining length of ribbon around the edge of the base board using a glue stick. Stack the tiers centrally on the base board, following the technique on page 141.

3 Melt the cocoa butter in a saucer over a dish of freshly boiled water and blend with the turquoise powder dust. Paint the 3-sided lotus-leaf design randomly over the entire cake, keeping the leaves close together.

4 Fit the piping bag with the icing nozzle and fill with gold royal icing. Pipe around the outline of each lotus design and add curly stems to fill spaces. Pipe pearls in between the design to give the cake an encrusted look. Leave to dry.

5 Dissolve the gold lustre in the alcohol dipping solution and use a fine paintbrush to lustre all of the hand-piped detail, including the pearls (see detail on page 81).

VERSAILLES BIRDS

By complete contrast to the monochrome designs in this book, this cake is richly painted with bright, vivid, tropical colours, inspired by the bold and expressive designs of Matthew Williamson and Alexander McQueen. I have dressed this cake with fresh anemones, guelder rose and green chrysanthemums.

YOU WILL NEED

10cm (4in), 18cm (7in) and 25cm (10in) square cakes

10cm (4in), 18cm (7in), 25cm (10in) and 33cm (13in) thick square cake boards

marzipan, for the cakes (see page 129 for quantities)

eau de nil sugar paste, for the cakes and base board (see pages 130 and 131 for quantities)

3.4m (3¾ yards) deep red ribbon 15mm (⅝in) wide, cut into 40cm (16in), 70cm (28in), 1m (39in) and 1.3m (52in) lengths

sharp scissors

royal icing (see page 133), for fixing

glue stick

tracing paper and pen

scribe

40g (1½oz) cocoa butter

wide range of powder dusts

fine paintbrushes

10cm (4in) polystyrene block 2.5cm (1in) deep

10 dowels

floristry wires, cut into 3

anemones, guelder rose and chrysanthemum pom poms

1 Place the cakes on thick cake boards of the same size and cover with marzipan and eau de nil sugar paste, following the techniques on pages 128 and 130–1. Cover the largest board (the base board) with sugar paste, following the technique on page 130. Leave the cakes and board to firm overnight.

2 Wrap a length of ribbon around the base of each tier, trim neatly and hold in position with a dab of royal icing. Fix the remaining length around the edge of the base board using a glue stick.

3 Trace the designs from the template on page 156 and scribe them onto the cakes, altering the angles and combinations of elements to create variety.

4 Melt the cocoa butter in a saucer over a dish of freshly boiled water. Prepare a palette of powder dusts, mix a little cocoa butter into each and use these to paint the design. Leave to dry.

5 Block the base tier with flowers, following the technique on page 140. Stack the top 2 tiers on the base tier, following the technique on page 141, but offset towards a corner. Dress the top tier to finish.

TREE OF LIFE

The tree of life is a powerful symbol that appears throughout many different cultures and religions, often relating to immortality or fertility. This striking design was inspired by a glass etching by René Lalique, and its strong lines and eye-catching monochrome scheme create a cake that needs no embellishments.

YOU WILL NEED

15cm (6in), 23cm (9in) and 30cm (12in) round cakes

15cm (6in), 23cm (9in), 30cm (12in) and 38cm (15in) thick round cake boards

marzipan, for the cakes (see page 129 for quantities)

sugar paste, for the cakes and base board (see pages 130 and 131 for quantities)

1.2m (4ft) black ribbon 15mm (⅝in) wide

glue stick

12 dowels

tracing paper and pen

scribe

25g (1oz) cocoa butter

black powder dust

paintbrush

2.25m (2½ yards) black ribbon 9mm (⅜in) wide, cut into 50cm (20in), 75cm (30in) and 1m (39in) lengths

sharp scissors

royal icing (see page 133), for fixing

1 Place the cakes on thick cake boards of the same size and cover with marzipan and sugar paste, following the techniques on pages 128 and 130–1. Cover the largest board (the base board) with sugar paste, following the technique on page 130. Leave the cakes and board to firm overnight.

2 Fix the piece of 15mm (⅝in) ribbon around the edge of the base board using a glue stick. Stack the tiers centrally on the base board, following the technique on page 141.

3 Trace the design from the template on page 151 and scribe this on to the cake, starting on the base tier and working up and over the cake onto the top of the top tier.

4 Melt the cocoa butter in a saucer over a dish of freshly boiled water. Blend with a little black powder dust and use this to paint the design. Leave to set.

5 Use the scribe to work over the design, etching the detail onto the cake. Wrap a length of 9mm (⅜in) ribbon around the base of each tier, trim neatly and hold in position with a dab of royal icing.

MONOCHOCCO SCROLLS

A monochrome scheme can be created effectively by working with white and dark chocolate. Here I have used vertical alternating chocolate scrolls blocked with hand-moulded dark chocolate roses and leaves to fashion a design that is both contemporary and chic. It is ideal for serving as a puddding at a wedding.

1 Place the cakes on thick cake boards of the same size and cover with white chocolate plastique, following the technique for marzipan on page 128. Cover the largest board (the base board) with dark chocolate plastique, following the technique for sugar paste on page 130. Leave the cakes and board to firm.

2 Fix the piece of ribbon around the edge of the base board using a glue stick. Place the base tier on the base board. Fill the piping bag with melted chocolate. Snip the end with sharp scissors and pipe a generous trail of white chocolate on one side of the cake.

3 Place the white and dark chocolate scrolls alternately in position, ensuring they are flush with the base board. Continue around the base tier, using 160 scrolls, then repeat with the middle and top tiers, using 120 and 80 scrolls respectively.

4 Use the remaining dark chocolate plastique to make 100 hand-moulded roses, following the technique on page 136, and 100 rose leaves, using the leaf veiner and cutter, following the technique in step 3 on page 110.

5 Prepare the tiers for blocking with the chocolate flowers, following the technique on page 140, but do not add the flowers in step 3. Stack the tiers into position, using some icing on top of each polystyrene block to hold the tier above in position. Build a small dome of white chocolate plastique 12cm (5in) in diameter and 5cm (2in) tall and place this on the top tier.

6 Using melted white chocolate to hold them in position, place the dark chocolate roses and leaves in the gaps between the tiers and over the dome on the top tier.

YOU WILL NEED

15cm (6in), 23cm (9in) and 30cm (12in) square cakes

15cm (6in), 23cm (9in), 30cm (12in) and 38cm (15in) thick square cake boards

white chocolate plastique (see page 135), for the cakes (see page 129 for quantities), plus 150g (5½oz) for the dome

2 quantities dark chocolate plastique (see page 136), for the base board (see page 131 for quantity), roses and leaves

1.5m (5ft) dark brown grosgrain ribbon 15mm (⅝in) wide

glue stick

piping bag

150g (5½oz) white chocolate, melted

sharp scissors

180 white chocolate scrolls

180 dark chocolate scrolls

4cm (1¾in) rose-leaf plunger veiner and cutter

8 dowels

12cm (5in) and 20cm (8in) polystyrene blocks 2.5cm (1in) deep

royal icing (see page 133), for fixing

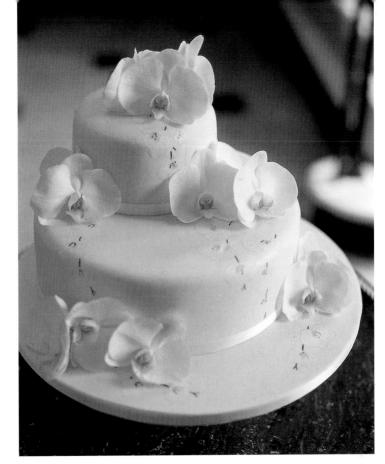

YOU WILL NEED

15cm (6in) and 30cm (12in) round cakes

15cm (6in), 30cm (12in) and 45cm (18in) thick round cake boards

marzipan, for the cakes (see page 129 for quantities)

eau de nil sugar paste, for the cakes and base board
(see pages 130 and 131 for quantities)

tracing paper and pen

scribe

25g (1oz) cocoa butter

white, yellow, fuchsia, green and brown powder dusts

paintbrushes

2.95m (3⅛ yards) white ribbon 15mm (⅝in) wide, cut into
50cm (20in), 1m (39in) and 1.45m (57in) lengths

royal icing (see page 133), for fixing

glue stick

12 dowels

Phalaenopsis orchids

SPRING ORCHID *Hand-painted orchids combine beautifully with fresh Phalaenopsis orchids, with their beautiful colouring and delicate structure, although you could use any combination of painted and fresh flowers. The design is clean, simple and fresh – perfect for a small informal spring wedding.*

1 Place the cakes on thick cake boards of the same size and cover with marzipan and sugar paste, following the techniques on pages 128 and 130–1. Cover the largest board (the base board) with sugar paste, following the technique on page 130. Leave the cakes and board to firm.

2 Place the base tier offset on the base board. Trace the design from the template on page 154 and scribe this onto the tiers and base board.

3 Melt the cocoa butter in a saucer over a dish of freshly boiled water. Prepare a palette of powder dusts, mix a little cocoa butter into each and use these to paint the design. Leave to dry.

4 Wrap a length of ribbon around the base of each tier, trim neatly and hold in position with a dab of royal icing. Also, fix the remaining length of ribbon around the edge of the base board using a glue stick.

5 Stack the top tier on the bottom one, following the technique on page 141, but offset. Dress the cake with fresh *Phalaenopsis* orchids.

ENCHANTED PEARL

In 2007, London's Victoria and Albert Museum held an Age of Couture exhibition, where I spotted a pair of gorgeous shoes: sage-green silk stippled with moss green with detailed gold filigree thread, fully encrusted with coral and saffron pearls and beads. They were the inspiration for this enchanted, vibrant cake.

YOU WILL NEED

15cm (6in) and 25cm (10in) square cakes

15cm (6in), 25cm (10in) and 33cm (13in) thick square cake boards

marzipan, for the cakes (see page 129 for quantities)

sage green sugar paste, for the cakes and cake board (see pages 130 and 131 for quantities)

6 dowels

2.9m (3⅛ yards) gold ribbon 15mm (⅝in) wide, cut into 60cm (24in), 1m (39in) and 1.3m (52in) lengths

glue stick

10g (¼oz) cocoa butter

2 tsp moss green powder dust

flat stippling brush

sharp scissors

1 quantity royal icing (see page 133), divided into 3 and coloured with concentrated edible food colours as follows: ⅓ old gold, ⅓ coral and ⅓ saffron yellow

3 piping bags

no. 1.5 (x 2) and no. 2 icing nozzles

2 tsp gold lustre

1 tbsp alcohol dipping solution

small paintbrush

gloriosa lilies, Orange Juice roses and foliage

1 Place the cakes on cake boards of the same size and cover with marzipan and sage green sugar paste, following the techniques on pages 128 and 130–1. Cover the largest board (the base board) with sugar paste, following the technique on page 130. Leave the cakes and board to firm overnight.

2 Place the base tier on the base board and stack the top tier on top, following the technique on page 141 but offset towards a back corner. Fix the 1.3m (52in) length of ribbon around the board using a glue stick.

3 Melt a little of the cocoa butter by placing it on a saucer over a bowl of freshly boiled water. Add the moss green powder dust and blend together, then use the stippling brush to paint this mixture over the entire cake to form the darker detail. Wrap the remaining lengths of gold ribbon around the base of each tier, trim neatly and hold in position with a dab of royal icing.

4 Fit one of the piping bags with one of the no. 1.5 nozzles and fill with gold royal icing. Pipe a filigree of gold over the entire cake. Blend the gold lustre with the alcohol dipping solution and paint over the gold filigree piping. Fit another piping bag with the no. 2 nozzle and fill with coral royal icing. Randomly pipe pearls over the entire cake. Repeat for the saffron pearls, using the remaining icing bag and no. 1.5 nozzle.

5 Place the hand-tied flowers on top.

seasonal

BASKET WEAVE

A single cake can be sufficient for a more intimate wedding, and I have shown here how it can be presented to maximum effect. Woven leather is popular for handbags, shoes and belts, so for this design I have decorated the cake with an intricate basket weave in royal icing, with seasonal ways of dressing it.

YOU WILL NEED

23cm (9in) round cake

2 x 23cm (9in) thin round cake boards

marzipan, for the cake
(see page 129 for quantity)

sugar paste, for the cake and board
(see pages 130 and 131 for quantities)

30cm (12in) thick round cake board

1 quantity royal icing (see page 133)

scribe

2 piping bags

nos. 3 and 19B icing nozzles

1m (39in) ribbon 15mm (⅝in) wide:
white for spring; pink for summer;
burnt orange for autumn;
sage green for winter

glue stick

seasonal flowers and cake stands:
spring – white roses, freesias and
paper-white narcissi presented on a
white cake stand; summer – pink roses
and guelder rose set on a plinth
decorated with similar fresh flowers;
autumn – Orange Brandy and Vandella
roses and oak leaves presented on a
glass cake stand; winter – Grand Prix
roses, calla lilies and berried ivy
presented on a black glass stand

1 Place the cake on one of the thin cake boards and cover with marzipan and sugar paste, following the techniques on pages 128 and 130–1. Cover the thick cake board (the base board) with sugar paste, following the technique on page 130. Leave the cakes and board to firm overnight.

2 Fix the cake to the covered board with a dab of royal icing. Place the other thin board centrally on top of the cake and scribe around it, then remove the board.

3 Fit the piping bags with the icing nozzles and fill both with royal icing. Begin with the no. 3 nozzle and pipe a vertical line from the top circle mark to the board.

4 With the no. 19B nozzle, pipe a 2cm (¾in) flat basket-weave section horizontally across the vertical line. Leave a 1cm (½in) space below this line and then repeat with another basket-weave section. Continue to the base of the tier.

5 Pipe the next vertical line 1cm (½in) away from the first, just overlapping the end of the basket-weave sections. Pipe the next line of basket-weave sections horizontally between the previous ones, in the spaces. Continue around the entire cake like this. Finish by piping a trail of pearls around the base of the cake. Fix a length of the relevant-coloured ribbon around the edge of the base board using a glue stick.

6 Dress the cake and present on a stand to fit the season.

SPRING RAIN

I was inspired by a bridal gown from the Rosa Clara collection for this cake. Vertical drops of white spring blossom flowers made from sugar are interspersed with clusters of white pearls. I have blocked the tiers with white roses and paper-white narcissi. The design is contemporary, romantic, clean and fresh.

YOU WILL NEED

15cm (6in), 20cm (8in) and 25cm (10in) round cakes

15cm (6in), 20cm (8in) and 25cm (10in) thick round cake boards

marzipan, for the cakes (see page 129 for quantities)

sugar paste, for the cakes (see page 131 for quantities)

100g (3½oz) white petal paste

5-petal blossom cutter, 1.5–2cm (⅝–¾in) in diameter

small ball tool

sponge mat

15cm (6in), 20cm (8in) and 25cm (10in) thin round cake boards

scribe

ruler

piping bag

no. 2 icing nozzle

1 quantity royal icing (see page 133)

1.95m (2¼ yards) white ribbon 15mm (⅝in) wide

10cm (4in) and 15cm (6in) polystyrene columns 5cm (2in) deep

30 white roses (see page 145) and 2 bunches paper-white narcissi

10 floristry wires, cut into 3

8 dowels

38cm (15in) diameter white cake stand

1 Place the cakes on thick cake boards of the same size and cover with marzipan and sugar paste, following the techniques on pages 128 and 130–1. To make the spring blossom flowers, roll out the petal paste very thinly and cut out 200 flowers with the 5-petal blossom cutter. (The paste dries out very quickly, so work only a little at a time.) Using the small ball tool and the sponge mat, draw the petals towards the centre of the blossom. Leave the cakes and flowers to firm overnight.

2 Place a thin board of the same size on the top of each tier and scribe around each to mark a circle on the top. With a ruler, mark 5cm (2in) intervals around each tier and scribe vertical lines at each mark to the top circle line. Wrap a length of ribbon around the base of each tier, trim neatly and hold in position with a dab of icing.

3 Fit the piping bag with the icing nozzle and fill with royal icing. Use 5 blossoms per vertical drop and ice these into position slightly randomly and just either side or on top of the pre-marked line, then pipe a pearl in the centre of each blossom.

4 Pipe clusters of pearls between the flowers from the top mark to the base and over the ribbon (see detail on page 98). Continue in this way until all the tiers are decorated.

5 Block the tiers with the flowers, following the technique on page 140 and interspersing the roses and narcissi. Dress the top tier to finish.

SUMMER GARLANDS

This wedding cake with pillars is quite traditional, but the garlands of sugar icing like folds of cloth give it a contemporary feel. The design is reminiscent of a Jenny Packham-style wedding gown, and I have dressed the cake with white lilies, lily of the valley and white roses — the epitome of scented summer flowers.

YOU WILL NEED

15cm (6in), 23cm (9in) and 30cm (12in) hexagonal cakes

15cm (6in), 23cm (9in), 30cm (12in), 38cm (15in) and 45cm (18in) thick hexagonal cake boards

marzipan, for the cakes
(see page 129 for quantities)

ivory sugar paste, for the cakes and base boards (see pages 130 and 131 for quantities), plus 1kg (2¼lb), for the garlands

6m (6½ yards) ivory ribbon 15mm (⅝in) wide

glue stick

ivory royal icing (see page 133), for fixing

icing sugar, for dusting

rolling pin

sharp knife

2.5cm (1in) flat paintbrush

piping bag

sharp scissors

54 ivory sugar rosebuds with green calyx
(see page 145)

6 dowels

6 x 8cm (3in) ivory pillars

8 white Casablanca lilies, 20 Bianca roses and 2 bunches lily of the valley

1 Place the cakes on thick cake boards of the same size and cover with marzipan and ivory sugar paste, following the techniques on pages 128 and 130–1. Cover the 2 largest boards (the base boards) with ivory sugar paste, following the technique on page 130. Leave the cakes and boards to firm overnight.

2 Fix a length of ribbon around the edge of both base boards using a glue stick, then fix the boards together with a dab of royal icing. Position the base tier on the stacked base boards. Wrap a length of ribbon around the base of each tier, trim neatly and hold in position with a dab of icing.

3 For the garlands, knead the remaining ivory sugar paste until smooth and pliable. On a clean work surface lightly dusted with icing sugar, roll out the paste to a depth of 3mm (⅛in). Measure the length of one hexagonal side on the base tier and use this as a guide. Cut a rectangle of paste the same length as the hexagonal panel x 8cm (3⅓in) high. Fold and pinch the sugar paste rectangle at the ends to create a garland.

4 Use a paintbrush to dampen the side of the cake with water where the garland is to be fixed and carefully place it in position. Repeat until you have made garlands for all the sides of the base tier, then make garlands for the smaller tiers, keeping their height at 8cm (3⅓in).

5 Fill a piping bag with ivory royal icing and snip the end with sharp scissors. Pipe a small amount of icing on the back of the rosebuds and fix 3 at the top of each garland (see detail on page 99).

6 Prepare the tiers for pillars, following the technique on page 142, then stack the cakes. Tuck the fresh flower heads between the pillars to dress.

TIP

Make the garlands one at a time and keep the sugar paste in a sealed polythene bag to prevent it drying out and cracking.

CONTEMPORARY ROMANTIC

Sometimes the simplest of cakes can be the most effective. This three-tier square cake is completely plain, effectively forming a backdrop to the flowers and so allowing them to shine through. I have showcased four contrasting designs and colours chosen here to complement the different seasons.

YOU WILL NEED

15cm (6in), 23cm (9in) and 30cm (12in)
square cakes

15cm (6in), 23cm (9in) and 30cm (12in) thick
square cake boards

marzipan, for the cakes
(see page 129 for quantities)

ivory sugar paste, for the cakes
(see page 130 for quantities)

8 dowels

10cm (4in) and 12cm (5in) polystyrene blocks
5cm (2in) deep

floristry wires, cut into 3

1 Place the cakes on thick cake boards of the same size and cover with marzipan and ivory sugar paste, following the techniques on pages 128 and 130–1. Leave the cakes to firm overnight.

2 Block the tiers with the appropriate seasonal flowers – green *Cymbidium* orchids for spring; peonies, ranunculus and wired butterflies for summer; Orange Juice roses, ranunculus and dried lavender for autumn; berried ivy and purple anemones for winter – following the technique on page 140. Dress the top tier to finish.

AUTUMN CHOCOLATE GANACHE AND FIGS

Aphrodite was the Greek goddess of love, beauty and fertility, and this decadent cake, made using the chocolate truffle torte recipe on page 146, is packed with the aphrodisiac temptations of chocolate and figs. Rich and seductive, it makes the perfect pudding at an autumnal wedding served with more figs and a poached pear sorbet.

YOU WILL NEED

15cm (6in), 25cm (10in) and 35cm (14in) round cakes

15cm (6in), 25cm (10in), 35cm (14in) and 45cm (18in) thick round cake boards

chocolate ganache buttercream, for the cakes (see page 137 for quantities)

6 quantities chocolate ganache (see page 137), for the cakes and base board

ladle

palette knife

1.45m (57in) dark brown ribbon 15mm (⅝in) wide

glue stick

12 dowels

piping bag

no. 5 icing nozzle

20 fresh figs

30 fresh sage leaves

1 Place the cakes on thick cake boards of the same size and cover the tops and sides with buttercream.

2 Before applying the first coat of ganache, place the cakes in the freezer for 15 minutes. Remove one cake from the freezer and place on a wire rack over a large sheet of non-stick baking paper. While the chocolate ganache is still just warm, generously ladle some over the cake so that it covers the top and gently runs down over the sides. Circle the base of the ladle over the ganache to encourage it to move outwards and downwards. Firmly grasp the wire rack and gently tap the rack up and down on the work surface to level the ganache and remove air bubbles.

3 Remove the cake from the wire rack and leave to set at room temperature. Remove the next cake from the freezer, place on the rack and repeat the process, reworking the excess ganache from the baking paper. Finally, coat the third cake.

4 Chill the cakes for 15 minutes again. Reheat the remaining ganache either in a microwave for 30 seconds or over a pan of simmering water. Remove one cake from the freezer and place it on the wire rack. Ladle ganache onto the cake and use a palette knife to spread it over the top and down the sides. Remove the cake from the wire rack and leave to set at room temperature. Repeat with the other cakes, again reworking the excess ganache from the baking paper, then cover the largest cake board (the base board) too and, when dry, fix the ribbon around the edge of the board using a glue stick. Place the leftover ganache in a lidded container.

5 Stack the tiers centrally on the covered base board, following the technique on page 141. Warm the remaining ganache as before until it is smooth, glossy and spoonable. Fit the piping bag with the icing nozzle and fill with the remaining ganache. Pipe large beads around the base of each tier. Dress the cake with fresh figs and sage leaves.

TIP

For a smoother or firmer finished cake (especially if you choose to prepare this cake for a summer wedding), replace the first coat of chocolate ganache with a layer of white chocolate plastique (see page 135).

AUTUMNAL CANDY STRIPE
Our candy striped wedding cake has become an international bestseller, and these smart individual versions on their iced stand are just as iconic – so Paul Smith with their vertical stripes in three colours. Each cake is topped with a hand-moulded sugar rose and piped green leaves – perfect for an autumn wedding.

YOU WILL NEED

15cm (6in) round cake

15cm (6in) thin round cake board

35 x 5cm (2in) round cakes (see page 132 for cutting instructions)

marzipan, for all the cakes (see pages 129 and 132 for quantities)

ivory sugar paste, for all the cakes and the stand (see pages 130, 132 and 139 for quantities)

20cm (8in), 25cm (10in), 30cm (12in) and 35cm (14in) thick round cake boards

3.6m (4 yards) sage green ribbon 15mm (⅝in) wide

10cm (4in), 12cm (5in) and 15cm (6in) polystyrene blocks 7.5cm (3in) deep

7m (7½ yards) ivory ribbon 15mm (⅝in) wide

350g (12oz) apricot sugar paste

350g (12oz) burnt orange sugar paste

1 quantity royal icing (see page 133), divided into 4 and coloured with concentrated edible food colours as follows: ¼ apricot, ¼ burnt orange and ½ sage green

4 piping bags

3 x no. 3 icing nozzles

silicone parchment paper cut into 35 x 7.5cm (3in) squares

sharp scissors

hypericum berries and Leonida roses

1 Put the large cake on a thin board. Cover all the cakes with marzipan and ivory sugar paste, following the techniques on pages 128, 130–1 and 132. Construct a 4-tier iced stand using the cake boards, ivory sugar paste, sage green ribbon, polystyrene blocks and ivory ribbon listed left, following the technique on page 139 to the end of step 4. Leave the cakes and stand to firm overnight.

2 Make 35 hand-moulded sugar roses (17 apricot and 18 burnt orange) following the technique on page 136. Set aside to firm. Fit 3 of the piping bags with icing nozzles and fill each with a different-coloured icing. Place each individual cake on a parchment paper square and the top tier on the smallest covered cake board. Pipe alternating coloured vertical lines from the top to the base of each cake.

3 Fill the remaining piping bag with sage green icing and snip a V at the end of the piping bag. With an up-and-down motion, pressure-pipe 3 green leaves on the top of each individual cake.

4 Set a hand-moulded rose in the centre of the leaves and leave to set.

5 Place the little cakes on the lower 3 tiers of the stand. Assemble the stand following step 5 on page 139 and place the 15cm (6in) cake on the top tier. Dress between the cakes with fresh hypericum berries and dress the top tier with fresh roses and berries to finish.

WINTER SNOWFLAKES

Winter weddings are becoming more popular, and for this cake I wanted to show an alternative to the traditional Christmas colours of white, dark green and red. These positively icy square cakes have been covered in either lilac or rich purple sugar paste, then decorated with jewelled snowflakes in purple and silver.

YOU WILL NEED

15cm (6in) round cake

15cm (6in) thin round cake board

35 x 5cm (2in) square cakes (see page 132 for cutting instructions)

marzipan, for all the cakes (see pages 129 and 132 for quantities)

lilac and purple sugar paste, for half the cakes each and also the large cake (see pages 130 and 132 for quantities)

23cm (9in), 28cm (11in), 33cm (13in) and 38cm (15in) thick round cake boards

lilac sugar paste, for the stand (see page 131 for quantities)

14.55m (16 yards) purple ribbon 15mm (⅝in) wide

10cm (4in), 12cm (5in) and 15cm (6in) polystyrene columns 7.5cm (3in) deep

3 piping bags

nos.1.5 and 2 (x 2) icing nozzles

1 quantity royal icing (see page 133), divided into 3 and coloured with concentrated edible food colours as follows: ⅓ grey, ⅓ lilac and ⅓ purple

3.9m (4¼ yards) lilac ribbon 15mm (⅝in) wide

sharp scissors and scribe

1 tsp silver lustre

2 tsp alcohol dipping solution

paintbrush

1 Put the large cake on a thin board. Cover all the cakes with marzipan and sugar paste, following the techniques on pages 128, 130–1 and 132. Prepare a 4-tier iced stand, using the cake boards, sugar paste, 10.95m (12 yards) of the purple ribbon and polystyrene columns listed left, following the technique on page 139 to the end of step 4. Leave the cakes and stand to firm overnight.

2 Fit the piping bags with the icing nozzles and fill with royal icing as follows: no. 1.5 wih grey, no. 2 with lilac and no. 2 with purple. Wrap the remaining purple ribbon around the base of 18 small cakes and the lilac ribbon around the base of 17 small cakes and the large cake, trim neatly and hold in position with a dab of icing.

3 On the top tier, pipe a collection of trees randomly around the side of the cake and top some with a piped star, using the 1.5 nozzle and grey icing.

4 Trace the snowflake design from the template on page 152 and use this as a guide to mark the 6 points of the snowflake on the top of each small cake with a scribe. Pipe a grey pearl in the centre, then work outwards with the pearl design, using purple on the lilac cakes and lilac on the purple. Leave to set.

5 Dissolve the silver lustre in the alcohol dipping solution and paint the mixture onto all the grey trees and pearls.

6 Place the little cakes on the lower 3 tiers of the stand, alternating the colours, and with all the ribbon joins facing inwards. Assemble the stand and place the 15cm (6in) cake on the top tier.

TIP

The alcohol dipping solution evaporates as you use it, so you may need to add more as you paint.

WINTER TRICOLOUR ROSEBUD

Chocolate has an affinity with winter weddings — lashings of rich dark chocolate truffle torte layered with chocolate ganache buttercream and covered in smooth chocolate. For this winter wedding cake I have tiered white, milk and dark chocolate and dressed the cake with clusters of tricolour chocolate rosebuds and leaves.

YOU WILL NEED

10cm (4in), 18cm (7in) and 25cm (10in) round cakes

10cm (4in), 18cm (7in) and 25cm (10in) thick round cake boards

white chocolate plastique (see page 135), for the first coat on all the cakes and the second coat on the top tier (see page 129 for quantities), plus 75g (3oz) for the rosebuds and leaves

milk chocolate plastique (made by mixing white and dark chocolate plastique [see page 136] together), for the second coat on the middle tier (see page 129 for quantities), plus 75g (3oz) for the rosebuds and leaves

dark chocolate plastique, for the second coat on the base tier (see page 129 for quantities), plus 75g (3oz) for the rosebuds and leaves

sharp knife

icing sugar or cocoa powder, for dusting

rolling pin

2cm (¾in) rose-leaf plunger veiner and cutter

50g (2oz) each white, milk and dark chocolate

3 piping bags

35cm (14in) cream grosgrain ribbon 15mm (⅝in) wide

55cm (22in) brown grosgrain ribbon 15mm (⅝in) wide

80cm (32in) dark brown grosgrain ribbon 15mm (⅝in) wide

sharp scissors

12 dowels

25cm (10in) diameter glass cake stand

1 Place the cakes on thick cake boards of the same size and cover with a first coat of white chocolate plastique and a second coat of the relevant chocolate plastique, following the techniques for marzipan and sugar paste on pages 128 and 130–1. Leave the cakes to firm overnight.

2 To make the rosebuds, warm a hazelnut-size piece of chocolate plastique in your hands. Roll into a ball and flatten with the base of your hand to a diameter of 3cm (1¼in). Gently curl and roll the disc into a rosebud and trim the base with a sharp knife. Repeat to make 15 of each colour chocolate.

3 On a clean work surface lightly dusted with icing sugar or cocoa powder, depending on which colour plastique you are using, roll out the remaining plastique to a depth of 2mm (⅛in). Use the rose-leaf plunger veiner and cutter to mark and stamp out the rose leaves. Pinch the base of each leaf and curl gently downwards to create shape and movement. Repeat to make 15 of each colour chocolate. Leave to firm.

4 Melt the 3 chocolates separately and pour into 3 separate piping bags. Wrap a length of same-colour ribbon around the base of each tier, trim neatly and hold in position with a dab of melted chocolate of the same colour. Stack the cakes centrally, following the technique on page 141. Use the corresponding melted chocolate to fix clusters of rosebuds and leaves on each tier to decorate. Present the cake on a cake stand.

mementoes

CAMELLIA

These cakes were inspired by Coco Chanel and the iconic Chanel camellia. I was announced as the Harper's Bazaar and Chanel Entrepreneur of the Year in 2006 and have become very interested in the history of the House of Chanel. These monochrome designs would be the perfect memento for a chic bridal shower.

YOU WILL NEED (PER CAKE)

5cm (2in) round cake
(see page 132 for cutting instructions)

60g (2¼oz) marzipan

75g (2¾oz) black or plain sugar paste

20cm (8in) black ribbon 15mm (⅝in) wide

20cm (8in) silver ribbon 6mm (¼in) wide

sharp scissors

royal icing (see page 133), for fixing

30g (1oz) black or white petal paste

icing sugar, for dusting

small rolling pin

2cm (¾in) rose-petal cutter

sugar glue

1 Cover each cake with marzipan and the black or plain sugar paste, following the technique on page 132, and leave to firm overnight.

2 Wrap a length of black ribbon overlaid with a length of silver ribbon around each cake, trim neatly and secure with a dab of royal icing.

3 To make the camellias, knead the petal paste until soft and pliable. On a clean work surface lightly dusted with icing sugar, roll out the paste to a depth of 2.5mm (⅛in). Cut out 11 petals using the rose-petal cutter. Roll one of them to form a central bud.

4 On 4 of the petals, use the sharp end of the cutter to nick a small amount from the opposite rounded edge and gently soften these edges by rubbing them with your finger.

5 Dab the pointed edge of each petal with sugar glue and fix evenly around the central bud. Gently curl these petals outwards.

6 Apply the second layer of 6 petals beneath the first layer, overlapping as they go around. Again, gently curl these outwards so that the tips are flush with the work surface. Leave to firm, then fix each camellia into position on a cake with a dab of icing.

GOLD-PAINTED ROSES
These cakes remind me of heavily gilded Versace designs, with their air of refined opulence. I have served these cakes on gold plates, with gold pastry forks and golden goblets of Champagne. The design would transpose well to the use of other bold colours, such as purple or black, for different wedding schemes.

YOU WILL NEED (PER CAKE)

5cm (2in) round cake
(see page 132 for cutting instructions)

60g (2¼oz) marzipan

75g (2¾oz) red sugar paste

20cm (8in) gold ribbon 15mm (⅝in) wide

PLUS

sharp scissors

1 quantity royal icing (see page 133), coloured with concentrated gold edible food colour

tracing paper and pen

scribe

piping bag

no. 2 icing nozzle

½ tsp gold lustre

1 tsp alcohol dipping solution

paintbrush

1 Cover each cake with marzipan and red sugar paste, following the technique on page 132, and leave to firm overnight.

2 Wrap a length of gold ribbon around each cake, trim neatly and secure with a dab of gold royal icing.

3 Trace the design from the template on page 155 and scribe it onto the top of each cake. Alternatively, set the stencil next to you as a guide and pipe freehand, so each design is individual.

4 Fit the piping bag with the icing nozzle and fill with gold royal icing. Pipe the outline of the rose and leave to set.

5 Dissolve the gold lustre in the alcohol dipping solution and paint the rose outline with lustre. (Note that this amount of lustre paste will be sufficient to paint 15–20 cakes.)

BLACK TIE

As their name suggests, these cakes would be the perfect memento for a black-tie wedding. I have presented them here in two colourways: black ribbon and bow for the gentlemen and pink ribbon and bow for the ladies. Thin ribbon bows are used by a number of designers, including Anya Hindmarch and Vera Wang.

YOU WILL NEED (PER CAKE)

5cm (2in) round cake
(see page 132 for cutting instructions)

60g (2¼oz) marzipan

75g (2¾oz) sugar paste

20cm (8in) black or pale pink ribbon
25mm (1in) wide

small sharp scissors

royal icing (see page 133), for fixing

ribbon insertion tool

45cm (18in) black or pale pink ribbon
3mm (⅛in) wide

1 Cover each cake with marzipan and sugar paste, following the technique on page 132, and leave to firm overnight.

2 Wrap a length of 25mm (1in) black or pink ribbon around the bottom of each cake, trim neatly and secure with a dab of royal icing.

3 Use the ribbon insertion tool to insert regular slits around each cake, 2cm (¾in) apart, directly above the ribbon. Make a ribbon bow from the length of 3mm (⅛in) ribbon, then snip the remainder into 2cm (¾in) lengths.

4 Use the ribbon insertion tool to tuck one end of the ribbon into the first slit, then the other end into the next slit. Repeat around the entire cake.

5 Fix the ribbon bow in position centrally on top of the cake with royal icing.

TRINKET BOXES
Beautiful jewels make beautiful mementoes, but if we can't all have a beautiful Boodles cocktail ring, as I have shown here, at least you can present your guests with individual trinket-box cakes. These were inspired by Tiffany and Co. but can be recreated in a spectrum of colours to complement any wedding.

YOU WILL NEED (PER CAKE)

5cm (2in) square cake
(see page 132 for cutting instructions)

70g (2½oz) marzipan

100g (3½oz) blue sugar paste

PLUS

icing sugar, for dusting

pastry brush

brandy

sharp knife

piping bag

no. 3 icing nozzle

1 quantity royal icing (see page 133)

1 Cover each cake with marzipan, following the technique on page 132. Knead the blue sugar paste until smooth and pliable.

2 On a clean work surface lightly dusted with icing sugar, roll out the sugar paste to a depth of 2.5mm (⅛in) and cut a 25 x 5cm (10 x 2in) strip. Brush the sides of the cake with brandy and wrap the sugar paste strip around it. Trim the excess vertically with a sharp knife to make a neat join at the back.

3 Roll out the excess paste to form an 8cm (3in) square, then cut out a 1cm (½in) square from each corner.

4 Brush the top of the cake and the top 1cm (⅜in) of the sugar-paste coated sides of the cake with brandy and place the lid in position. Gently pinch the corners to create a neat box shape.

5 Fit the piping bag with the icing nozzle and fill with royal icing. Pipe a line from the base of the lid on one side to the opposite side, then repeat with the other 2 sides. Finally, pipe a bow in the centre with 2 tails. Set aside to dry.

CAN CAN

Our larger Cannes Cannes wedding cake has been such a huge favourite with our clients that it made perfect sense to create these individual cakes in a similar design, finished with a ribbon and bow to complement. These frou frou cakes, with their appealing frills, can also be made using chocolate plastique.

YOU WILL NEED (PER CAKE)

5cm (2in) square cake
(see page 132 for cutting instructions)

70g (2½oz) marzipan

170g (6oz) sugar paste

icing sugar, for dusting

small rolling pin

pastry brush

brandy

sharp knife

paintbrush

40cm (16in) ribbon 9mm (⅜in) wide

royal icing (see page 133), for fixing

1 Cover each cake with marzipan and half the sugar paste, following the technique on page 132, and leave to firm overnight.

2 Knead the remaining sugar paste until smooth and pliable. On a clean work surface lightly dusted with icing sugar, roll out the sugar paste to a depth of 2.5mm (⅛in). Cut a strip 25 x 7cm (10 x 2¾in) – or 15mm (⅝in) taller than the covered cake – and use the edge of a small rolling pin to gently feather one of the long edges. Brush the sides of the cake with brandy and wrap the sugar-paste strip around, feather edge upwards. Trim the excess vertically with a sharp knife to make a neat join at the back.

3 Roll out the excess paste to the same depth and cut into 8 x 2cm (3 x ¼in) strips. Gently gather one of the strips to make a ruffle frill.

4 Dampen the top of the cake with water, using a paintbrush, and place the frill in position. Gather more of the strips and put the frills in place until the top is filled.

5 Make a ribbon bow from the length of ribbon. Wrap the remaining ribbon around the base of the cake, trim neatly and secure with a dab of royal icing, then fix the bow in position with more icing.

TIP

For less sugar paste on the cake, omit the first coat of white sugar paste. Instead cut a 5.5cm (2¼in) square of sugar paste and place this on the top of the marzipanned cake to act as a lid held in position with brandy. Continue with rolling out the collar for each cake.

BOOTS AND HANDBAGS

What is couture without the obligatory accessories of handbag and shoes to complete an outfit – or indeed to inspire one? While not technically cakes, these cookies are extremely chic in every way: killer-heel boots to rival any Jimmy Choo or Christian Laboutin creations and a contemporary handbag to match.

YOU WILL NEED

150g (5½oz) unsalted butter, softened

150g (5½oz) golden caster sugar

1 egg, beaten

300g (10½oz) plain flour, sifted, plus extra for dusting

zest from 2 lemons

50g (1¾oz) ground almonds

½ tsp almond essence

tracing paper and pen

stiff card

small sharp scissors

small sharp knife or craft knife

1 quantity royal icing (see page 133), divided into 3 and coloured with concentrated edible food colours as follows: ½ fuchsia, ¼ black and ¼ left white

4 piping bags

2 x no. 1.5 icing nozzles

fine paintbrush

1 To make the cookie dough, beat together the butter and sugar until light and fluffy. Add half the egg and beat again, then stir in the remaining ingredients. Gather up the dough and wrap in cling film, then place in the fridge to rest for 20 minutes.

2 Preheat the oven to 180°C (350°F), fan oven 160°C (325°F), gas mark 5. Trace the designs from the templates on page 154 and transfer onto stiff card, then cut out for use as stencils.

3 On a work surface lightly dusted with flour, roll out the cookie dough to a depth of 2.5mm (⅛in) and put the stencils on top. Use a small sharp knife or craft knife to cut around them, reversing the boot templates every other time in order to create pairs. Cut out 20 pairs of boots and 20 handbags. Place the cookies on a non-stick baking tray and bake for 8 minutes until golden, then transfer carefully onto a wire rack to cool.

4 Thin half the fuchsia royal icing and all the white royal icing to a flooding consistency with water (see page 133). Fit 2 of the piping bags with the icing nozzles and fill one with fuchsia piping icing and one with black piping icing. Pipe the outlines of the boots and bags, including the curly handles for the bags.

5 Fill the remaining 2 piping bags with the flooding icing, one fuchsia and one white, and snip the ends with sharp scissors. Flood the boots and bags outlines, using a paintbrush to nudge the icing into all the corners. Set aside to skin over.

6 Finally, use the remaining black piping icing to pipe the flap and clasp on the handbags and the studs and laces on the boots. Leave to set firm, then store in an airtight container until needed.

TIP

The cookie dough can be frozen for up to 1 month double-wrapped in cling film. Allow to defrost in the fridge overnight. Once baked, the cookies will keep fresh in an airtight container for 12 days but are best eaten within 2–3 days.

techniques
recipes and templates

TECHNIQUES

These techniques will help you with covering your baked cakes in preparation for the decorative techniques shown in the chapters, as well as assembling the tiers. There are recipes for icings and fillings, and instructions on making and wiring edible and fresh flowers. Most cakes should be covered the day before you start the final decoration, to provide a firm surface to work on.

COVERING A CAKE WITH MARZIPAN

It is essential to cover your cake with marzipan or chocolate plastique first. Their function is three-fold: being oil-based they lock in moisture, they provide a firm, smooth base for a smart finish with your top coat and they prevent the colour of the cake leaching into the icing.

FOR UNDER SUGAR PASTE

For a layer under sugar paste, the marzipan is rolled out and smoothed over the cake in one piece to create softly rounded edges.

YOU WILL NEED

cake

thin or thick cake board of the same size as the cake (see method)

pastry brush

boiled, sieved apricot jam

marzipan (see opposite for quantities)

icing sugar, for dusting

rolling pin

smoother

sharp knife

turntable or bowl

1 Place the cooled cake upside down on a cake board and brush liberally with boiled, sieved apricot jam. (Note that if the cake is going to be placed on a base board for display, as on page 130, then the cake board can be thin; otherwise it should be thick to give stability for stacking or blocking the cake.)

2 Knead the marzipan until smooth and pliable. Dust a clean work surface lightly with icing sugar and roll the marzipan evenly into a size large enough to cover the top and sides of the cake, allowing for surplus (use string to measure). The marzipan should be approximately 5mm (¼in) thick. Carefully lift the marzipan onto the cake.

3 Smooth the top and sides of the cake using your hands and a smoother. Trim off most of the excess marzipan with a sharp knife.

4 Lift the cake and board onto a turntable or upturned bowl and neatly trim the remaining excess marzipan, keeping it flush with the bottom of the board.

FOR UNDER ROYAL ICING

Cakes covered with royal icing should have sharp, clean, angular edges, and so the marzipan needs to be rolled out and applied as separate pieces. This method is more time consuming, but the finished result is well worth it.

YOU WILL NEED

cake

base board (thick cake board
7.5cm/ 3in larger than the cake)

pastry brush

boiled, sieved apricot jam

marzipan (see below for quantities)

icing sugar, for dusting

rolling pin

sharp knife

1 Place the cooled cake upside down in the centre of the cake board and brush liberally with boiled, sieved apricot jam. Knead the marzipan until smooth and pliable. Dust a clean work surface lightly with icing sugar and roll the marzipan evenly into a size large enough to cut out the top and sides separately and accurately (use string or a ruler to measure), using a sharp knife. The marzipan should be approximately 5mm (¼in) thick.

2 Using both hands, carefully lift the marzipan onto the cake. Fix the top in position first, then apply each of the sides in turn. Trim any excess. Leave to set overnight before applying the royal icing (see page 134).

TIP If the cake is very domed, slice the peak off to level the surface before you turn the cake upside down. You can roll a thin sausage of marzipan and use this to build up any uneven edges around the base of the cake once it is on the cake board.

guide to quantities to cover cakes with marzipan/chocolate plastique

● round cake ■ square cake

size of cake	10cm	10cm	15cm	15cm	20cm	20cm	23cm	23cm	25cm	25cm	30cm	30cm	35cm	35cm	40cm	40cm
	(4in) ●	(4in) ■	(6in) ●	(6in) ■	(8in) ●	(8in) ■	(9in) ●	(9in) ■	(10in) ●	(10in) ■	(12in) ●	(12in) ■	(14in) ●	(14in) ■	(16in) ●	(16in) ■
quantity	400g	500g	600g	750g	800g	1kg	1kg	1.25kg	1.25kg	1.5kg	1.75kg	2kg	2.25kg	2.65kg	2.85kg	3kg
	(14oz)	(1lb 2oz)	(1lb 5oz)	(1lb 10oz)	(1lb 12oz)	(2lb 4oz)	(2lb 4oz)	(2lb 12oz)	(2lb 12oz)	(3lb 8oz)	(3lb 8oz)	(4lb 8oz)	(5lb)	(5lb 13oz)	(6lb 4oz)	(6lb 10oz)

COVERING A BASE BOARD AND/OR A CAKE WITH SUGAR PASTE

Rolled out and smoothed over a cake, sugar paste creates a fast, clean, smooth finish with gently curved edges. It provides a good base for decoration or looks fabulous simply adorned with flowers. It is soft and pliable, sets firm but not rock hard and cuts easily.

guide to quantities to cover cakes with sugar paste ● round cake ■ square cake

size of cake	15cm (6in) ●	15cm (6in) ■	20cm (8in) ●	20cm (8in) ■	23cm (9in) ●	23cm (9in) ■	25cm (10in) ●	25cm (10in) ■	30cm (12in) ●	30cm (12in) ■	35cm (14in) ●	35cm (14in) ■	40cm (16in) ●	40cm (16in) ■
quantity	750g (1lb 10oz)	850g (1lb 14oz)	1kg (2lb 4oz)	1.25kg (2lb 12oz)	1.25kg (2lb 12oz)	1.5kg (3lb 8oz)	1.5kg (3lb 8oz)	1.8kg (4lb)	2.1kg (4lb 10oz)	2.35kg (5lb 3oz)	2.7kg (6lb)	3kg (6lb 10oz)	3.25kg (7lb 3oz)	3.5kg (7lb 11o)z

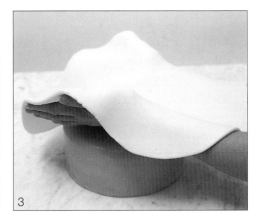

YOU WILL NEED

base board (a thick cake board 7.5cm/3in larger than the cake)

pastry brush

cooled boiled water

icing sugar, for dusting

sugar paste (see opposite for quantities)

rolling pin

smoother

sharp knife

cake placed on a thin board of the same size and marzipanned (see page 128)

brandy (optional)

turntable or bowl

royal icing (see page 133), for fixing

palette knife

1 To cover a base board, brush it with cooled boiled water. On a clean work surface lightly dusted with icing sugar (too much will dry the sugar paste), knead the sugar paste until smooth and pliable. Roll the paste evenly to the correct size – large enough to cover the board and roughly 3mm (⅛in) thick. Carefully place the paste over the board and use a smoother to finish. Hold the board in one hand and use a sharp knife to cut away the excess, keeping the knife flush with the side of the board. Leave to set (ideally overnight).

2 To cover a marzipan- or chocolate plastique-covered cake, brush the cake with brandy or cooled boiled water. This acts as a good antiseptic seal between the marzipan and sugar paste as well as being an adhesive.

3 On a clean work surface lightly dusted with icing sugar, knead the paste until smooth and pliable. Roll the paste evenly into a size large enough to cover the top and sides of the cake, allowing for surplus (use string to measure). It should be approximately 5mm (¼in) thick. Carefully lift the paste onto the marzipan-covered cake.

guide to quantities to cover base boards with sugar paste/chocolate plastique

size of board	18cm (7in) ●	18cm (7in) ■	20cm (8in) ●	20cm (8in) ■	23cm (9in) ●	23cm (9in) ■	25cm (10in) ●	25cm (10in) ■	28cm (11in) ●	28cm (11in) ■	30cm (12in) ●	30cm (12in) ■	33cm (13in) ●	33cm (13in) ■	35cm (14in) ●	35cm (14in) ■
quantity	315g (11oz)	400g (14oz)	420g (15oz)	525g (1lb 3oz)	550g (1lb 4oz)	675g (1lb 8oz)	650g (1lb 7oz)	825g (1lb 13oz)	800g (1lb 12oz)	1kg (2lb 4oz)	950g (2lb 2oz)	1.2kg (2lb 12oz)	1.2kg (2lb 12oz)	1.4kg (3lb 2oz)	1.3kg (3lb)	1.6kg (3lb 8oz)

size of board	38cm (15in) ●	38cm (15in) ■	40cm (16in) ●	40cm (16in) ■	45cm (18in) ●	45cm (18in) ■	50cm (20in) ●	50cm (20in) ■	55cm (22in) ●	55cm (22in) ■
quantity	1.5kg (3lb 5oz)	1.9kg (4lb 3oz)	1.7kg (3lb 12oz)	2.1kg (4lb 8oz)	2.2kgg (5lb)	2.7kg (6lb)	2.6kg (5lb 12oz)	3.3kg (8lb 12oz)	3.2kg (6lb 15oz)	4kg (9lb)

4 Smooth the top and sides with your hands, carefully pressing the sugar paste against the cake. Be careful not to drag the icing down the sides of the cake, as this will cause it to crack and tear.

5 Use a smoother to give the cake a professional, clean finish and prick any air bubbles with a pin. Trim most of the excess sugar paste away from the cake.

6 Lift the cake onto a turntable or upturned bowl and neatly trim away all the excess sugar paste using a sharp knife, keeping the knife flush with the bottom of the thin board.

7 Put a dab of royal icing on the covered base board. Slide a palette knife carefully underneath the cake and thin board and lift from underneath using both hands. Carefully set the cake in position on the base board.

COVERING SMALL CAKES WITH MARZIPAN

Individual cakes need to be covered with marzipan and sugar paste before they are decorated. Small round cakes are stamped out from a large cake with a 5cm (2in) cutter; 5cm (2in) square cakes are cut from a large cake with a sharp knife. Use one layer of a chocolate or lime and coconut cake, split and filled; half a fruit or sticky date cake; or half a lemon or carrot cake, split and filled.

1 Brush the cake sides and top with boiled, slightly cooled apricot jam.

2 Roll out the marzipan (60g/2¼oz per round cake; 70g/2¾oz per square cake) to 3mm (⅛in) thick and cut into 15cm (6in) squares. Place a square over each cake and press down all the way round.

3 Carefully position a 6cm (2⅜in) cutter over the cake and stamp out. Remove the excess marzipan. Use 2 straight-edge smoothers together to flatten the top and neaten the sides and base edge.

COVERING SMALL CAKES WITH SUGAR PASTE

Once they have been covered with either a layer of marzipan or a layer of white chocolate plastique (for those people who dislike marzipan), small cakes are covered with a top coat of sugar paste. This will set firm overnight to allow handling and additional decoration. Allow 75g (3oz) sugar paste per 5cm (2in) round cake and 85g (3½oz) per 5cm (2in) square cake.

1 Brush the marzipan-covered cakes with brandy or cooled boiled water.

2 Roll out the sugar paste to 3mm (⅛in) thick and cut into 20cm (8in) squares. Place a square over each cake and press down all the way around.

3 Carefully position a 7.5cm (3in) cutter over the cake and stamp out. Remove the excess sugar paste. Use 2 straight-edge smoothers together to flatten the top and neaten the sides and base edge.

ROYAL ICING

Royal icing is not only traditional – it is also staging a comeback! Made from fresh egg white and icing sugar, royal icing is a sweet paste that is lathered onto the cake and allowed to set. Once made, royal icing will keep fresh in an airtight container for up to 7 days, though it will separate if left for longer than 24 hours and should be rewhisked before using. To colour royal icing, dip a cocktail stick into the required concentrated food colour, then add to the icing and blend.

yields 400g (14oz)
YOU WILL NEED (FOR PIPING)

1 medium egg white

350g (12oz) icing sugar, sifted

juice ½ lemon, sieved through a tea strainer

Place the egg white in a clean, grease-free bowl and whisk until it forms very soft peaks. Add the icing sugar and whisk slowly at first until all the sugar is incorporated, then on full speed for 1 minute until it is glossy. Add the lemon juice and whisk for another minute.

yields 400g (14oz)
YOU WILL NEED (FOR COVERING)

1 medium egg white

350g (12oz) icing sugar, sifted

1 tsp glycerine

Make as for piping icing, adding glycerine instead of lemon juice. This will allow the icing to be cut without splintering.

TIP Reconstituted albumen powder can be substituted for fresh egg white and is available from specialist cake suppliers. It should be used according to the manufacturer's instructions, but the ratio is generally 25g (1oz) albumen powder and 150ml (5fl oz) water to 900g (2lb) icing sugar.

FLOODING ICING

Flooding icing is used to fill the royal iced outlines for making run-outs.

To make flooding icing, you need to thin royal icing down with drops of egg white or water. (Egg white will make the finished run-out stronger, but the icing may take longer to dry. Water will enable it to dry faster, but it will be less strong.) Add the chosen liquid a drop at a time and stir gently. Do not beat the icing, as you will incorporate too much air and bubbles will appear in the run-outs. To assess when the icing is of the right consistency, stir it and then count how long it takes for the ripples to subside. If it takes 10 seconds, then the icing is ready – any more, and it is a bit stiff; any less and it is a bit runny.

COVERING A CAKE WITH ROYAL ICING

Covering a cake with royal icing is a much more laborious technique than using sugar paste, as several coats are required to build the icing up to the desired thickness. It sets very firm and is somewhat brittle to slice, but the finished icing has a wonderfully sweet flavour and a clean, architectural finish that is perfect for particular designs, for example Antique Rose (see page 48).

YOU WILL NEED

palette knife

royal icing (see page 33)

marzipan-covered cake on a base board (a thick cake board 7.5cm/3in larger than the cake)

side and top scrapers

sharp knife

1 Use a palette knife to apply the icing liberally onto one of the sides of the cake, using a paddling motion to expel any air bubbles from the icing.

2 Hold a side scraper at a 45-degree angle to the cake and steadily and purposefully pull it towards you. Use a sharp knife in a downward motion to remove the excess icing from the 2 side ends and top edge. Repeat on the opposite side. Allow the icing to set for at least 8 hours before repeating the process on the other 2 sides.

3 Spread the royal icing liberally on the top of the cake. Using a long scraper and holding the ends away from the cake, carefully pull the scraper at an angle of 45 degrees across the top of the cake towards you. Use a sharp knife to trim the edges. Allow to set for 8 hours in a warm, dry environment. Repeat steps 1–3 until all the sides and the top have received 3 coats.

4 To cover the board, spread the royal icing onto each side in turn and, holding a side scraper at a 45-degree angle to the board, carefully pull it towards you. Clean the edges with a sharp knife.

guide to quantities to cover cakes with royal icicng   ● round cake ■ square cake

size of cake	15cm (6in) ●	15cm (6in) ■	20cm (8in) ●	20cm (8in) ■	23cm (9in) ●	23cm (9in) ■	25cm (10in) ●	25cm (10in) ■	30cm (12in) ●	30cm (12in) ■	35cm (14in) ●	35cm (14in) ■	40cm (16in) ●	40cm (16in) ■
quantity	800g (1lb 12oz)	1kg (2lb 4oz)	1kg (2lb 4oz)	1.25kg (2lb 12oz)	1.25kg (2lb 12oz)	1.5kg (3lb 8oz)	1.5kg (3lb 8oz)	1.75kg (3lb 14oz)	2kg (4lb 8oz)	2.25kg (5lb)	2.5kg (5lb 8oz)	2.7kg (6lb)	3kg (6lb 10oz)	3.25kg (7lb 3oz)

CHOCOLATE PLASTIQUE

Chocolate plastique is a combination of pure chocolate with a sugar stock syrup – effectively glucose – which makes chocolate malleable, enabling you to roll it out to cover a cake or hand mould it to create the fans, roses and leaves used in many of the designs shown here. It has all the taste of chocolate, but with the texture of sugar paste, and gives a smooth, firm finish to a cake. You can use chocolate plastique to cover a cake in exactly the same way as you would marzipan and sugar paste. To make milk chocolate plastique, knead together dark and white chocolate plastique.

PLASTIQUE STOCK SYRUP

yields 450ml (16fl oz)
YOU WILL NEED

250ml (9fl oz) water

140g (5oz) caster sugar

85g (3oz) glucose syrup

Place all the ingredients in a saucepan and bring to the boil. Remove from the heat and leave to cool. This recipe will provide slightly more than is necessary to create the white chocolate plastique recipe below.

WHITE CHOCOLATE PLASTIQUE

yields 2½kg (5lb 8oz)
YOU WILL NEED

1.75kg (3lb 12oz) white chocolate, broken into pieces

115g (4oz) cocoa butter

400g (14oz) glucose syrup

300ml (10½fl oz) plastique stock syrup

1 Melt the chocolate in a microwave or place it in a clean, heat-resistant bowl over a saucepan of simmering water. Melt the cocoa butter in a microwave or place it in a clean, heat-resistant bowl over a saucepan of simmering water. (It is important to melt the cocoa butter and chocolate separately, as they melt at different rates and both need to be melted for the recipe to work.) Mix the chocolate and cocoa butter together and stir well. Measure the glucose syrup and stock syrup together and warm slightly in the microwave. (This allows all the ingredients to be at a similar temperature for the final mix.)

2 Pour the chocolate mixture over the glucose and stock syrups and mix well with a wooden spoon until smooth. Transfer the mixture into a large clean freezer bag and leave overnight at room temperature to set.

3 When ready to use, knead the chocolate plastique until smooth and pliable, then roll out on a work surface lightly dusted with icing sugar.

DARK CHOCOLATE PLASTIQUE

This paste is quite firm and chewy. Use this recipe for making hand-moulded roses, lilies and other decorations, but mix it 1:1 with white sugar paste for covering cakes.

yields 2.25kg (5lb)
YOU WILL NEED

1.25kg (2lb 12oz) dark chocolate (55% maximum cocoa solids), broken into pieces

1kg (2lb 4oz) glucose syrup

1 Melt the chocolate in a microwave or place it in a clean, heat-resistant bowl over a pan of simmering water. Heat to 43°C (110°F). Heat the glucose syrup separately to the same temperature. Pour the syrup into the melted chocolate and stir with a wooden spoon until thoroughly combined. Allow to cool completely.

2 Transfer the mixture into a large clean freezer bag and leave overnight at room temperature to set. To use, peel away the bag and knead the chocolate until smooth and pliable, then roll out on a work surface lightly dusted with icing sugar.

HAND-MOULDED ROSES

These versatile and effective roses, which can be made from chocolate plastique or sugar paste, are ideal for wedding cakes. Use 20g (¾oz) for a small rose; 40g (1½oz) for a larger one.

1 Warm 1 quantity chocolate plastique between your palms and roll into a ball. (If using sugar paste, there is no need to warm it first.) Place between 2 sheets of plastic. Flatten quickly with the base of your palm, then, using your index finger, flatten two-thirds of the way around the ball, leaving a thicker base. Repeat to create 4 more petals.

2 Remove the petals from the plastic sheet and, holding one of the petals by the thicker base, gently roll it to form the centre of the rose.

3 Wrap a petal around the rose centre, then fix the final 3 petals so they overlap one another. Gently tease the petals into shape. Slice the base off the rose using a palette knife.

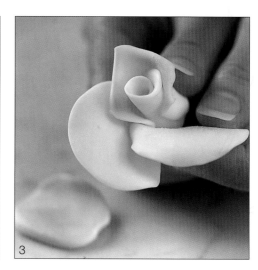

CHOCOLATE GANACHE

Chocolate ganache is a blend of boiled cream and chocolate. It has a smooth, rich, velvety texture that literally melts in the mouth. Mixed with buttercream, it becomes a wonderfully decadent filling or frosting.

yields 300g (10½oz)
YOU WILL NEED

175g (6oz) dark chocolate (70% cocoa solids), broken into pieces

125ml (4fl oz) double cream

Place the chocolate pieces in a clean, dry bowl. Bring the cream to the boil, remove from the heat and pour over the chocolate. Stir with a wooden spoon until the chocolate is melted and the ganache is smooth and glossy. Pour over the cake while still warm. Alternatively, leave to cool for 15 minutes before making chocolate ganache buttercream (see below).

size of cake	15cm (6in)	20cm (8in)	25cm (10in)	30cm (12in)	35cm (14in)
to sandwich 2 halves	½ quantity	1 quantity	1½ quantities	2 quantities	2½ quantities
to cover top and sides	½ quantity	1 quantity	1½ quantities	2 quantities	2½ quantities

BUTTERCREAM

Buttercream is a combination of softened unsalted butter and icing sugar. The basic mixture can be combined with other flavours such as lime and coconut, orange, lemon curd and chocolate ganache (see below).

yields 750g (1lb 11oz)
YOU WILL NEED

250g (9oz) unsalted butter, softened

500g (1lb 2oz) icing sugar, sifted

1 tsp Madagascan Bourbon vanilla extract

Beat the softened butter for 2 minutes using a wooden spoon or an electric hand-held mixer. Add the icing sugar and beat slowly at first, then add the vanilla extract and beat vigorously until the buttercream is very light and fluffy. Store any excess buttercream in the refrigerator for up to 2 weeks.

LIME AND COCONUT BUTTERCREAM

Mix together 60g (2¼oz) grated creamed coconut and the zest and juice of 2 limes. Microwave or place over a pan of simmering water until the coconut melts. Leave to cool. Beat 40g (1½oz) unsalted butter until smooth and creamy, then add 60g (2¼oz) icing sugar and whisk, slowly at first, then at full speed, until light and fluffy. Stir in the cooled coconut and lime mixture and whisk until light and marshmallowy.

FRESH ORANGE BUTTERCREAM

Stir the grated zest of 2 fresh oranges and 4 tbsp juice into 1 quantity buttercream. This buttercream works equally well layered in a vanilla cake or a chocolate-based cake.

LEMON CURD BUTTERCREAM

Stir 275g (9½oz) lemon curd into 1 quantity buttercream.

CHOCOLATE GANACHE BUTTERCREAM

Stir 1 quantity chocolate ganache into 1 quantity buttercream.

PIPING ICING

All of the iced designs in this book are created using royal icing (see page 133). Once you have made a piping bag, just slip a nozzle into the tip, fill with royal icing (coloured or plain white) and start piping.

MAKING A PIPING BAG

Piping bags are made from triangles of non-stick siliconized baking paper. Smaller sizes are good for flooding while larger ones are good for piping single colours onto a number of tiers.

1 Fold a 30–45cm (12–18in) square of paper in half diagonally to make 2 triangles and cut the paper in half along the crease. Place the paper on the table with the tip of the triangle facing you and bring the underside of the left point to the right of centre and hold with your thumb and forefinger.

2 Bring the right-hand point up, over and round to the back to meet at the centre.

3 Carefully fold the points of the paper over to secure the bag.

GLAZING

There are a number of lustres and edible gels available that can dramatically enhance elements of a hand-iced cake. Pearls can be brought to life with edible gel to maintain a dewy appearance, and whole sections of icing can be brushed with lustres mixed with alcohol dipping solution for an authentic sparkle.

EDIBLE GEL

Made from a sugar glucose solution, edible gel can be brushed neatly onto set icing to create an instant wet look. The gel remains slightly tacky even when set, so be careful when handling the finished cake.

EDIBLE GEL MIXED WITH LUSTRES

For Queen Elizabeth Diamond (see page 22), I mixed topaz lustre with edible gel to create a paste. I then brushed this mixture onto the pearls for an authentic dewy, pearly shine. Various colours of lustres are available, including ruby, sapphire, jade, copper and gold.

LUSTRES MIXED WITH ALCOHOL DIPPING SOLUTION

Lustres can also be dissolved in alcohol dipping solution and brushed onto set icing, as on Enchanted Pearl (page 90). The alcohol allows you to brush the lustre onto the icing detail (in this case gold filigree) but then evaporates, leaving a matt-sheen appearance. In Bows and Brooches (page 42), the lustre is painted over the ribbons, the bow and its tails, as well as the brooch centre. Be careful, though, as the lustre will brush off or mark the cake if it is touched.

INDIVIDUAL CAKE STANDS

Small cakes presented on a stand are becoming increasingly popular and are an effective way to create height and drama for more intimate celebrations. Here I show how to make an iced display stand for small cakes. Stands can be made in many shapes and sizes – round, square and hexagonal are the most practical. Decide on the number and size of tiers and calculate the quantity of cakes you will need using the chart below.

ICED STAND

The individual iced cakes shown in this book are presented on iced stands. The colour of the icing and ribbon on the stand are co-ordinated with the cakes.

1 Lightly dust a work surface with icing sugar. Knead the sugar paste until pliable and smooth. Working on one of the cake boards at a time, roll out a piece of paste that is large enough to cover the board to a depth of 5mm (¼in).

2 Brush the board with cold water, then lift the icing over the board. Smooth the icing, then, holding the knife against the board, cut away the excess icing. Rub a glue stick around the edge of the board and attach a length of ribbon. Repeat for the other boards.

3 Rub glue over the polystyrene blocks (for a square stand) or columns (for a round stand) and wrap ribbon around them, starting at the bottom edge and working your way up, carefully overlapping as you go until you reach the top edge. Glue the final piece into place.

4 Fix each block or column to the board it will sit on with royal icing. Leave to set overnight.

5 When the cakes are in place, stack the tiers of the stand, securing the blocks or columns to the board above with royal icing to make the stand secure.

TIP Make your top tier no smaller than 20cm (8in) in diameter. This will allow the tier below to have a large enough block or column to support the top tier while still providing sufficient space to display the cakes.

YOU WILL NEED

icing sugar, for dusting

sugar paste (see page 131 for quantities)

rolling pin

thick cake boards

pastry brush

smoother

glue stick

15mm (⅝in) wide ribbon, to edge the boards and wrap around the central columns

polystyrene blocks or columns

royal icing, for fixing

guide to quantities to cover stands with sugar paste						● round stand ■ square stand
size of board	20cm (8in)	25cm (10in)	30cm (12in)	35cm (14in)	40cm (16in)	45cm (18in)
● 5cm (2in) diameter cakes	5	9	10	12	14	17
■ 5cm (2in) diameter cakes	8	12	12	16	20	24

BLOCKING A CAKE

Blocking a cake with fresh flowers or fruit is a stunning way to present it, creating an illusion that each tier is suspended on a bed of fruit or flowers. Blocking is also one of the most stable methods of stacking tiers. The polystyrene blocks provide surface-area stability for the tier above and also a base for wired flowers.

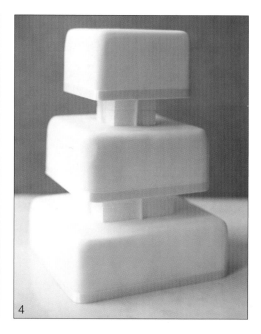

YOU WILL NEED

2 polystyrene blocks, 5cm (2in) deep and 10cm (4in) smaller than the middle and largest cakes

3 cakes placed on thick cake boards, then decorated and edged with ribbon (if using)

8 dowels

pen

ruler

sharp heavy-duty scissors or junior hacksaw

1 Place the polystyrene blocks in the centre of the 2 largest tiers. Insert a dowel at the centre point of each side of the block, making sure they are straight and pushed down to the boards. Mark each dowel where it meets the top of the block.

2 Remove the dowels and line them up on a table. The marks will be at slightly varying heights: measure the one with the highest mark and use a ruler and pen to re-mark each dowel to this point. (This will ensure the cake is level and supported when the dowels are reinserted and the next tier is stacked on top.) Cut each dowel to the new mark using heavy-duty scissors or a junior hacksaw. Replace the dowels in each cake so they are flush with the top of the blocks.

3 Prepare and add the flowers following the technique on page 145. (The flowers are not shown above so that the stacking can be seen clearly.)

4 Using both hands, gently lift the middle tier and position it carefully on the block of the base tier until it is central, stable and even. Repeat the process with the top tier, ensuring that the ribbon joins are at the back of the cake.

TIP Make sure that you scale the polystyrene blocks with the size of the tiers to maintain stability and to allow sufficient space for the flowers or fruit.

STACKING A CAKE

Stacking is a preferred American way to present a finished wedding cake. The tiers, which are stacked either centrally over each other or offset to one side or corner, are supported with hidden boards and dowels. The overall height of a stacked cake is less than that of other tiered cakes, so for a grander effect you can increase the number of tiers, including some false upper tiers if necessary.

YOU WILL NEED

12 dowels

3 cakes placed on thick cake boards, then decorated and edged with ribbon (if using)

pen

ruler

sharp heavy-duty scissors or junior hacksaw

royal icing (see page 133), for fixing

palette knife

1 Push 6 dowels randomly into the centre of the bottom tier, making sure their line does not fall outside the size of the tier to be stacked above. Use a pen to mark each dowel at the point where it surfaces from the cake. (For a large cake such as Queen Elizabeth Diamond you will need 8 dowels per tier.)

2 Remove the dowels and line them up on a table. Find the average mark and, using a ruler and pen, mark each of the dowels at the same point. (This will ensure the cake is level and supported when the dowels are reinserted and the next tier is placed on top.) Cut each dowel to the new mark using heavy-duty scissors or a junior hacksaw. Check that all the dowels are the correct length before reinserting them into the cake, as they will be very difficult to remove again. Once the dowels are pushed right into the cake, spread a small amount of royal icing on the centre of the cake with a palette knife.

3 Gently lift the middle tier and position it carefully on the base tier. Repeat step 2 with another 6 dowels on the middle tier before placing the top tier in position. Adjust the ribbons on the top tiers so they fit snugly against the lower tiers and the joins are at the back.

TIP Leave the cakes for 24 hours after decorating them before attempting to stack them. This allows time for the coverings to harden and set so that you will be able to handle the tiers without the icing cracking or dimpling.

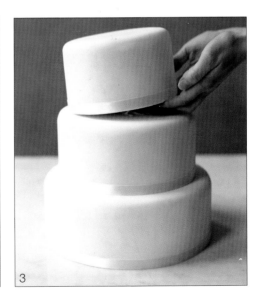

USING PILLARS TO SEPARATE TIERS

Separating tiers with pillars is a traditional way to add dramatic height and grandeur to a cake, and the space created between the tiers can be dressed with fresh, sugar or silk flowers. Pillars are available in many heights, colours and finishes – dowels placed inside the pillars carry all the weight of the tiers. With very large or heavy tiers, increase the number of pillars to up to eight on each tier.

YOU WILL NEED

grid template (see page 158)

3 cakes placed on thick cake boards, then decorated and edged with ribbon (if using)

scribe

6 dowels

6 x 9cm (3½in) pillars

ruler

pen

sharp, heavy-duty scissors or junior hacksaw

1 Place the grid template centrally over the largest cake. Select the relevant point to the cake size on a 'C' line and mark this with a scribe; mark the same point on the other 'C' line and the 'A/C' line.

2 Insert a dowel into each of the marked points and drop a pillar over the top. Place a ruler across 2 of the pillars and mark the dowels at the top of the pillars with a pen. Move the ruler around to between one of these pillars and the third one and finally between this pillar and the first one, marking the rods each time. Remove the pillars from the cake.

3 Remove the dowels and line them up on a table. Find the average mark and, using a ruler and pen, mark each of the dowels at this point. (This will ensure the cake is level and supported when the dowels are replaced and the next tier is stacked into position.) Cut each dowel to the new mark using heavy-duty scissors or a junior hacksaw. Replace the dowels in the cake and position a pillar carefully over each one. Repeat the above with the middle tier.

4 Finally, stack the tiers, making sure they are level, stable and centred, and that all the ribbon joins are at the back.

STACKING TIERS WITH A CENTRAL COLUMN

Separating cake tiers with a central column gives a contemporary, uncluttered look, and wrapping the column in a contrasting or complementary ribbon creates either a dramatic or more subtle effect. It's not necessary to add finishing touches between the tiers, so this technique is popular for designs that reach or cover the top of each tier so that they can be clearly seen.

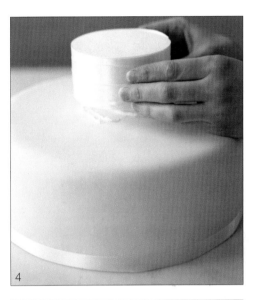

YOU WILL NEED

grid template (see page 158)

3 cakes placed on thick cake boards, then decorated and edged with ribbon (if using)

scribe

10 dowels

pen

ruler

sharp heavy-duty scissors or a junior hacksaw

2 polystyrene columns, 5cm (2in) deep and 10cm (4in) smaller than the medium-sized and largest cakes

ribbon 25mm (1in) wide to cover the polystyrene columns

glue stick

2 thin boards of the same size and shape as the polystyrene columns

royal icing (see page 133) , for fixing

1 Place the grid template centrally over the largest cake and mark the centre point on the cake with a scribe.

2 Insert a dowel into the cake at this point, making sure it is straight and pushed down to the board. Mark the dowel with a pen where it surfaces from the cake. Remove the dowel and line it up with 4 others. Use a ruler and pen to mark each dowel to the measured point. (This will keep the cake level and supported when the dowels are replaced and the tiers are stacked.)

3 Cut each dowel to the new mark using the scissors or hacksaw. Push the dowels into the cake, keeping them within the diameter of the column. Cover the largest column with ribbon, if using, wrapping it around several times to ensure the polystyrene is covered and securing it in position with a glue stick. Glue the column to a thin board (to prevent the dowels pushing up through the polystyrene under the weight of the cake). Spread a small amount of royal icing in the centre of the cake.

4 Carefully place the column on the cake (board side facing down) with the centre over the central dowel.

5 Repeat this process with the middle tier, then leave both tiers to set for 30 minutes Carefully stack the tiers, ensuring the ribbon joins are at the back.

SUGAR LILIES

Romantic lilies look stunning when used to dress a cake. Here I show you how to make them from petal paste, which will last long after the wedding day. If you want to make pure white lilies, as for Cascading Crystal Rose (see page 44), omit the dusting and painting stage.

YOU WILL NEED

lengths of 24-gauge wire, cut into 3

30g (1oz) white petal paste

knife

paintbrushes

green and pink powder dusts

large white lily stamens

green florist's tape

icing sugar, for dusting

small veining rolling pin

10cm (4in) lily cutter

lengths of 26-gauge wire, cut into 3

10cm (4in) lily-veining mould

soft foam pad

ball tool

brown liquid food colour

1 Bend the top of a length of 24-gauge wire over to form a small hook. Take a piece of white petal paste the size of a cherry tomato and form it into an elongated cone. Pinch the blunt end into 3 to form the end of the stigma and mark with a cross using a knife. Insert the hooked end of the wire gently into the thin end of the stigma and leave to dry overnight. The next day, brush the stigma with green powder dust. Position 6 large lily stamens around the stigma and tape into position with green florist's tape.

2 On a clean work surface lightly dusted with icing sugar, roll out the remaining petal paste thinly using the veining rolling pin. Place the lily cutter on the paste, centred over the thick vein marked by the rolling pin, and cut out 6 petals. Insert approximately 2cm (¾in) of a length of 26-gauge wire into the thick vein of each petal. Lay the wired petal inside the veining mould, with the wire facing outwards, and press the mould sides firmly together to indent the markings on the petal. Place each petal, in turn, on a foam pad and rub it gently with a ball tool, working from the centre outwards, to feather the edges of the lily gently and give the flowers a sense of movement.

3 Allow the lily petals to dry overnight propped over an upturned bowl so that the petals curve gently backwards. (For a more closed lily, dry the petals flat.) Dust the centre length of each petal with pink powder dust and use a paintbrush dipped into brown liquid food colour to paint small dots on top. Leave to dry.

4 Tape the first 3 petals evenly around the central stamens using florist's tape. Add the final 3 petals one at a time and fix in position with tape. Handle the lilies at the base where the wire is inserted, as this is the most stable point.

TIP You will need 6 petals for each lily, but, as they're very fragile, it is a good idea to make extra. If a petal snaps, pull it out gently and tape another into position.

SUGAR ROSEBUDS

Fingernail-sized rosebuds made of petal paste are delicate and effective yet simple to make. They can be made in more than one colour to add interest and contrast to a cake. They keep well if stored in a clean, dry container, so can be made well in advance.

YOU WILL NEED

15g (½oz) petal paste per rose –
10g (⅓oz) for the rose (yellow) and
5g (⅙oz) for the calyx (green)

icing sugar, for dusting

small rolling pin

3cm (1¼in) rose-petal cutter
(5 petals)

ball tool

soft foam pad

sugar glue

1.5cm (⅝in) calyx cutter

1 Form a pea-sized ball of yellow petal paste into a cone and allow to dry for 1 hour. On a clean work surface lightly dusted with icing sugar, roll out the remaining yellow petal paste and press the rose cutter onto it. Use the ball tool on the soft foam pad to gently soften and thin the edges of the petals.

2 Dab a small amount of sugar glue in the centre of the 5 petals and place the cone pointing upwards in the centre. Gather the first petal up and around the cone, then fold the remaining petals up, tucking each inside the next with one side free.

3 Roll out the green paste and cut out the calyx. Use the ball tool on the soft pad to gently thin and curl the fronds upwards. Dab the centre with sugar glue and set the rose in place.

PREPARING FLOWERS FOR BLOCKING

I like to dress cakes with fresh flowers. There are many varieties and colours available, so it is worth experimenting, but I have found roses to be particularly effective for blocking.

YOU WILL NEED

florist's scissors

fresh roses

floristry wires, cut into 3

polystyrene column(s) or block(s)
(5cm/2in deep if you want just 1 row
of flowers; 9cm/3½in deep
if you want 2 rows)

1 Trim each rose to leave approximately 2cm (¾in) of stalk. Gently tease a wire into the stalk.

2 Insert the wire into the polystyrene column or block. Repeat, working around the cake base or tier and ensuring the roses are lined up and equal. (If you are using 2 rows, position the upper row in between the flowers on the bottom row.) Don't underestimate the number of flowers you will need!

TIP The table below is provided as a guide only. The numbers will vary depending on the species of rose, how full blown the flowers are and how tightly you position them next to one another. You may like to include other flowers or greenery to fill any gaps and reduce the cost.

tier diameter	15cm (6in)	20cm (8in)	25cm (10in)	30cm (12in)	35cm (14in)	40cm (16in)
no. of roses required for 1 row	8	12	16	20	26	32
no. of roses required for 2 rows	14	22	30	38	50	60

CAKE RECIPES

Choose from chocolate truffle, luscious lemon, moist carrot, traditional fruit, sticky date and lime and coconut. Note that one quantity of cake mixture makes a 15cm (6in) round cake or a 12cm (5in) square/hexagonal cake; other sizes of cakes require multiples as shown in the charts on the right. Cooking times are given in each recipe, with individual increases or decreases for each 5cm (2in) variation on these standard tin sizes.

cake size	quantities	cake size	quantities
● 10cm (4in)	½	■● 10cm (4in)	½
● 12cm (5in)	¾	■● 15cm (6in)	1¼
● 18cm (7in)	1½	■● 18cm (7in)	1½
● 20cm (8in)	2	■● 20cm (8in)	2¼
● 23cm (9in)	2¼	■● 23cm (9in)	2¾
● 25cm (10in)	3	■● 25cm (10in)	3½
● 30cm (12in)	4	■● 30cm (12in)	5
● 35cm (14in)	5½	■● 35cm (14in)	7
● 38cm (15in)	6¼	■● 38cm (15in)	8
● 40cm (16in)	7	■● 40cm (16in)	9

● round cake   ■● square/hexagonal cake

ingredients for 15cm (6in) cake
200g (7oz) plain chocolate (70% cocoa solids), broken into pieces
250g (9oz) unsalted butter, softened
350g (12oz) light soft brown sugar
5 medium eggs, beaten
1½ tsp vanilla extract
140g (5oz) plain flour, sifted

bake: fan 140°C (275°F)
conventional 160°C (325°F) gas mark 3

CHOCOLATE TRUFFLE TORTE

This cake is made with melted chocolate and very little flour, and its texture is similar to that of a chocolate brownie. It's delicious sandwiched with chocolate ganache buttercream. Its low flour content means that this cake is best baked in two halves, then sandwiched together.

1 Preheat the oven. Have all the ingredients at room temperature. Melt the chocolate carefully in a microwave or in a bowl over simmering water, then leave to cool. Grease and line 2 deep cake tins with non-stick baking paper. Beat together the butter and sugar until light and fluffy, then add the beaten eggs, a little at a time, beating between each addition.

2 Pour the cooled melted chocolate slowly into the creamed mixture, beating all the time. Stir in the vanilla extract, then fold in the sifted flour.

3 Spoon the mixture evenly into the tins and bake for 45 minutes (plus or minus 20 minutes per 5cm/2in of tin size). The baked cakes should be well risen with a crust but should still wobble when shaken gently. Remove the cakes from the oven. Leave the cakes to cool in the tins, then remove. The crust will sink down into the cakes. Sandwich the cakes together with chocolate ganache buttercream (see page 137).

TO STORE This cake will keep for up to 10 days once covered and decorated or wrapped in greaseproof paper and kept in an airtight container. It is suitable for freezing, but needs to defrost overnight.

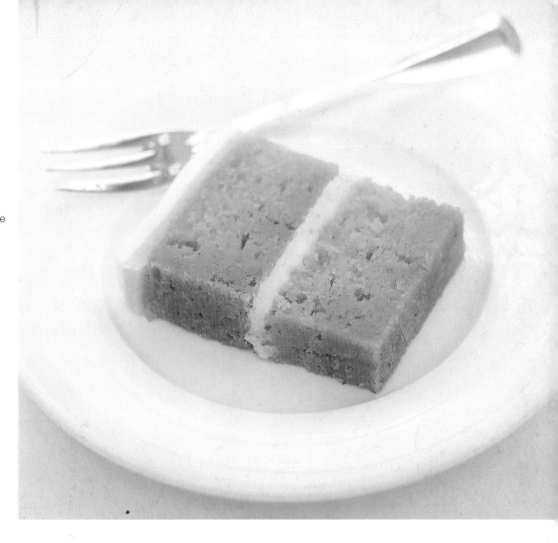

ingredients for 15cm (6in) cake

140g (5oz) self-raising flour

140g (5oz) plain flour

200g (7oz) unsalted butter, softened

200g (7oz) golden caster sugar

4 medium eggs, beaten

grated zest of 1 lemon and 2 tbsp juice

2 tsp vanilla extract

for the syrup glaze:

remainder of lemon juice (approx.
  100ml/3½fl oz)

85g (3oz) golden caster sugar

bake: fan 140°C (275°F)
conventional 160°C (325°F) gas 3

LUSCIOUS LEMON CAKE

This lemon cake recipe is light and refreshing, which makes it a lovely addition to a summer wedding
and perfect after a rich banquet. Slice it horizontally in half and fill with lemon curd buttercream, then
cover it with marzipan and icing or chocolate plastique. Although there are a lot of fresh lemons to zest
and squeeze, the finished cake is well worth the effort!

1 Preheat the oven. Have all the ingredients at
room temperature. Grease and line a deep cake tin
with non-stick baking paper. Sift the flours together.
Beat together the butter and sugar until light and
fluffy, then add the beaten eggs, a little at a time,
beating between each addition. Stir a few tablespoons
of flour into the creamed mixture to prevent it
curdling, then carefully fold in the remainder. Stir
in the lemon zest and juice and the vanilla extract.
Spoon the mixture into the prepared tin and bake
for 1 hour 25 minutes (plus or minus 15 minutes
per 5cm/2in of tin size) or until a skewer inserted
into the middle of the cake comes out clean.

2 While the cake is baking, make the syrup glaze.
Sieve the lemon juice into a small pan, add the
sugar, stirring all the time, and heat gently until
the sugar dissolves. Remove from the heat. Once
the cake is baked, remove from the oven and pierce
with a skewer several times. Spoon the lemon syrup
over the top. Leave the cake to cool in the tin,
then remove. Split and sandwich with lemon curd
buttercream (see page 137).

TO STORE This cake is best served and
eaten fresh but will keep for up to 5 days once
covered and decorated or wrapped in greaseproof
paper and kept in an airtight container. It is
suitable for freezing, but needs to defrost overnight.

ingredients for 15cm (6in) cake

25ml (1fl oz) dark rum

100g (3½oz) sultanas

175g (6oz) plain flour

2 tsp ground cinnamon

1 tsp ground nutmeg

1 tsp bicarbonate of soda

150ml (5fl oz) sunflower oil

75g (2½oz) golden caster sugar

75g (2½oz) light soft brown sugar

2 medium eggs, beaten

grated zest of 1 lemon

grated zest of 1 orange

175g (6oz) carrots, peeled and grated

55g (2oz) desiccated coconut

55g (2oz) walnuts, chopped

1 tsp vanilla extract

2 tsp chopped glacé ginger (optional)

for the citrus syrup:

75g (2½oz) light soft brown sugar

juice of 1 lemon

juice of 1 orange

bake: fan 140°C (275°F)

conventional 150°C (300°F) gas mark 2

MOIST CARROT CAKE

This carrot cake with added walnuts, rum-soaked sultanas and coconut makes a lovely, lighter alternative to a rich fruit cake. The cake is spiked with a citrus syrup to help keep it moist and fruity. It does not need filling, but some fresh orange buttercream adds a taste of luxury.

1 Pour the rum over the sultanas and leave to soak for 1 hour. Preheat the oven. Have all the ingredients at room temperature. Grease and line a deep cake tin with non-stick baking paper (which should stand at least 2cm/¾in above the tin to contain the lemon syrup in step 3). Sift the flour together with the ground cinnamon, ground nutmeg and bicarbonate of soda. Beat together the sunflower oil, both sugars and the eggs until smooth.

2 Stir the flour mixture into the smooth batter. Add the lemon and orange zests, grated carrot, desiccated coconut, walnuts, vanilla extract and chopped glacé ginger (if using) and stir well to combine. Spoon the mixture into the prepared tin and bake for 1½ hours (plus or minus 15 minutes per 5cm/2in of tin size) or until a skewer inserted into the middle of the cake comes out clean.

3 While the cake is baking, make the syrup. Place the sugar in a jug, then add the sieved lemon and orange juice. Stir well and continue to stir at intervals. Once the cake is baked, remove it from the oven and immediately pierce it with a skewer several times. Carefully spoon or pour over the citrus syrup. Leave the cake to cool in the tin, then remove. Split and sandwich with fresh orange buttercream (see page 137), if using.

TO STORE This cake keeps fresh for up to 14 days if covered and decorated with icing or wrapped in greaseproof paper and kept in an airtight container. It is suitable for freezing, but needs to defrost overnight.

TIP Once the citrus syrup is poured over, it will appear flooded. This is perfectly normal and all this delicious juice will gradually be absorbed into the cake.

TRADITIONAL RICH FRUIT CAKE

This moist cake contains dried dates, prunes and apricots alongside the more commonly used currants, raisins and sultanas, giving a flavour that is more pronounced and a little less sweet. The molasses gives a rich treacle flavour. Ideally, bake the cake 8 weeks in advance.

1 Combine the currants, sultanas, raisins, prunes, apricots, dates and glacé cherries with the brandy and the orange and lemon zest and juice. Leave to absorb for a minimum of 24 hours – ideally 72 hours.

2 Preheat the oven. Have all the ingredients at room temperature. Grease and line a deep cake tin with non-stick baking paper. Sift the flour together with the ground ginger, cinnamon and nutmeg. Beat together the butter and sugar until light and fluffy, then add the beaten eggs, a little at a time, beating between each addition.

3 Stir a few tablespoons of flour into the creamed mixture to prevent it curdling, then carefully fold in the remaining flour. Stir in the molasses, then the soaked fruit (reserving the brandy in which it has been soaked) and the chopped nuts.

4 Spoon the mixture into the prepared tin and bake for 3½ hours (plus or minus 15 minutes per 5cm/2in of tin size) or until a skewer inserted into the middle of the cake comes out clean. If the top of the cake appears to be browning too quickly, fold a sheet of greaseproof paper in half, cut a small hole the size of a walnut in the centre and carefully place it over the top of the cake. (Make sure you wear oven gloves to do so!)

5 Remove the cake from the oven. Leave the cake to cool in the tin, then remove. Brush the top with the reserved brandy, then wrap the cake in a double layer of greaseproof paper and a double layer of kitchen foil to store.

TO STORE This cake keeps fresh for up to 9 months if marzipanned and iced and kept in an airtight container in a cool, dry place. Undecorated, and wrapped in greaseproof paper and foil, it will keep for up to 3 months.

ingredients for 15cm (6in) cake

125g (4½oz) seedless currants
100g (3½oz) sultanas
100g (3½oz) Californian raisins
40g (1½oz) whole pitted prunes, snipped into 3
40g (1½oz) whole dried apricots, snipped into 3
40g (1½oz) whole pitted dates, snipped into 3
50g (2oz) natural-colour glacé cherries, chopped
75ml (2½fl oz) brandy (40% alcohol)
grated zest and juice of 1 lemon
grated zest and juice of 1 orange
175g (6oz) plain flour
1 tsp ground ginger
2 tsp ground cinnamon
1½ tsp ground nutmeg
125g (4½oz) unsalted butter, softened
125g (4½oz) light soft brown sugar
2 medium eggs, beaten
½ tbsp molasses
25g (1oz) chopped almonds

bake: fan 120°C (250°F)
conventional 140°C (275°F) gas mark 1

STICKY DATE CAKE

This cake is moist, sticky and full of flavour, and makes a welcome alternative to a traditional fruit cake. It stacks well and requires no filling, making it an ideal choice for the base tier of many of the cakes, though one can be added if wanted.

ingredients

160g (5½oz) pitted Medjool dates
160g (5½oz) unsalted butter,
  cut into pieces
240g (8½oz) light muscovado sugar
2 medium eggs
40g (1½oz) preserved stem ginger,
  chopped
grated zest of 1 lemon
1 tsp vanilla extract
200g (7oz) Bramley cooking apple, grated
160g (5½oz) self-raising flour, sifted

bake: fan 140°C (275°F)
conventional 160°C (325°F) gas mark 3

1 Preheat the oven. Have all the ingredients at room temperature. Grease and line a deep cake tin with non-stick baking paper.

2 Place the dates in a bowl and cover with boiling water. Melt the butter and sugar together in a large saucepan and leave to cool slightly.

3 Beat the eggs, ginger, lemon zest and vanilla extract into the butter and sugar. Drain the dates and chop finely. Add to the saucepan and mix well, then stir in the grated apple and flour. Spoon the mixture into the prepared tin and bake for 1 hour (plus or minus 15 minutes per 5cm/2in of tin size) or until a skewer inserted into the middle of the cake comes out clean with a few crumbs. Leave the cake to cool in the tin, then remove.

TO STORE Store in an airtight container for up to 1 week. It is suitable for freezing, but needs to defrost overnight.

LIME AND COCONUT CAKE

This beautiful fresh cake combines tart limes with creamy coconut. It is delicious at any time of the year, but its fresh, lively flavours make it ideal for a summer wedding. The addition of creamed coconut means that this cake is best baked in two halves, then sandwiched together.

ingredients

160g (5½oz) unsalted butter, softened
160g (5½oz) golden caster sugar
160g (5½oz) self-raising flour, sifted
3 medium eggs, beaten
1 tbsp milk
60g (2¼oz) creamed coconut, grated

bake: fan 170°C (340°F)
conventional 190°C (375°F) gas mark 5

1 Preheat the oven. Have all the ingredients at room temperature. Grease and line two deep cake tins with non-stick baking paper. Put all the cake ingredients into a large bowl and whisk together until you have a smooth batter.

2 Divide the mixture betweeen the two prepared tins, smooth the surface and bake in the oven for 20 minutes (plus or minus 15 minutes per 5cm/2in of tin size) until risen, light golden and the cakes spring back when pressed. Leave the cakes to cool a little, then remove from the tins and place on a wire rack to cool completely. Sandwich with lime and coconut buttercream (see page 137).

TO STORE Store in an airtight container and eat within 2 days. This cake is not suitable for freezing.

TEMPLATES

PETITE ROSE
See page 61

WINTER SNOWFLAKES
See page 109

TREE OF LIFE
See page 86

LACE VEIL
See page 54

COUTURE CONFETTI
See page 67

QUEEN ELIZABETH DIAMOND: 30cm (12in)
See page 22

VENETIAN
See page 29

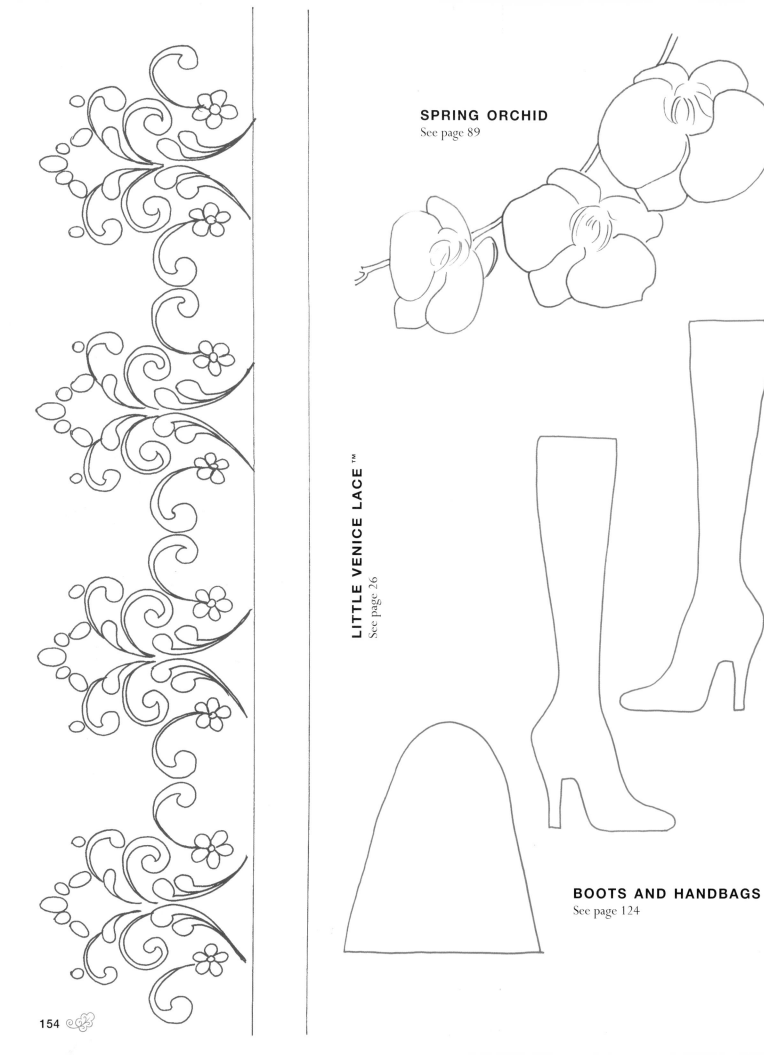

SPRING ORCHID
See page 89

LITTLE VENICE LACE ™
See page 26

BOOTS AND HANDBAGS
See page 124

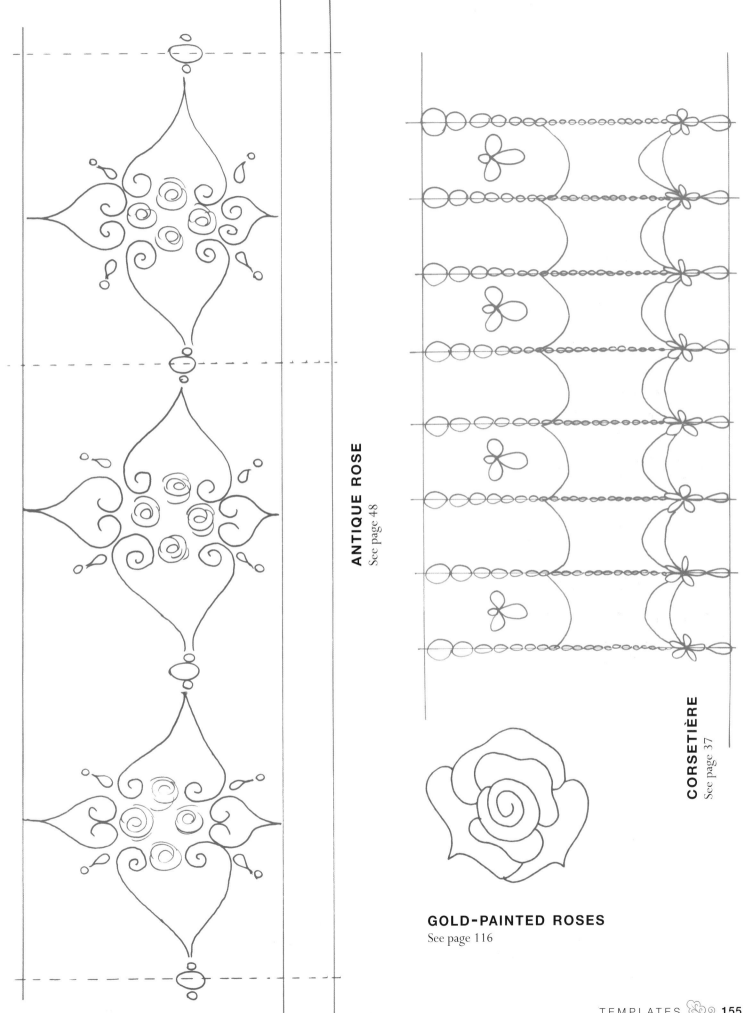

ANTIQUE ROSE
See page 48

CORSETIÈRE
See page 37

GOLD-PAINTED ROSES
See page 116

VERSAILLES BIRDS
See page 85

QUEEN ELIZABETH DIAMOND: 20cm (8in)
See page 22

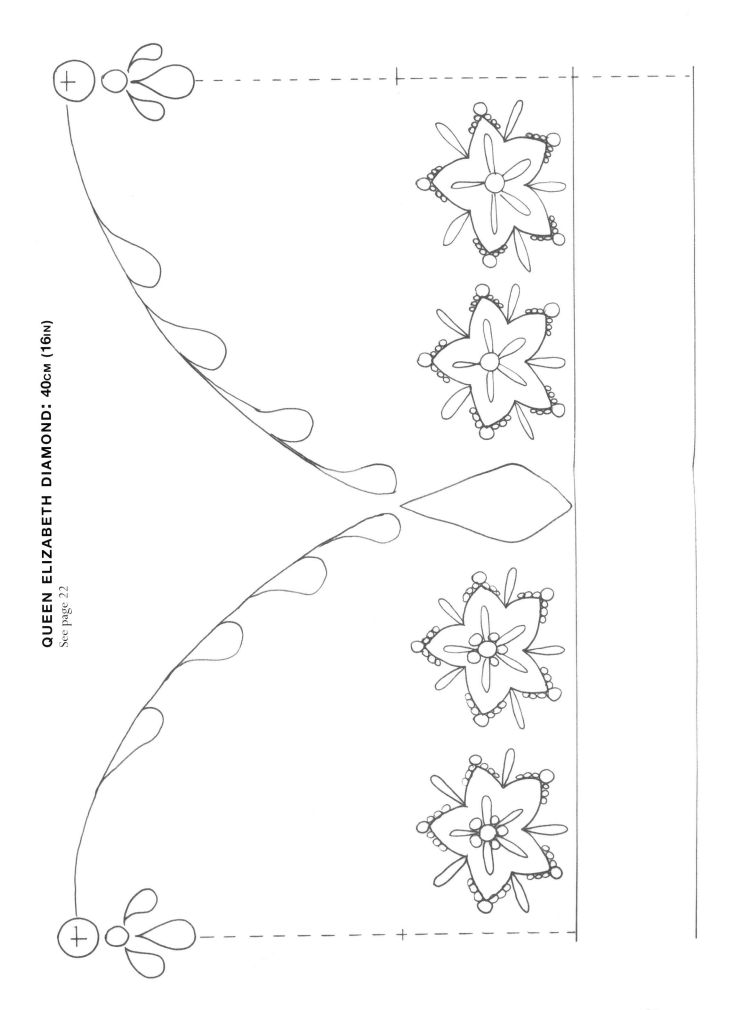

QUEEN ELIZABETH DIAMOND: 40cm (16in)
See page 22

MARKING PILLARS ON A CAKE

See pages 142 and 143

For round and square cakes up to 25cm (10in) use 4 pillars, positioned at **A** or **B**. For larger cakes use 8 pillars, positioned at **A** and **B**.

For hexagonal-shaped tiers use either 3 or 6 pillars, positioned at **C**, **D** or a combination of both.

25cm (10in) ca

23cm (9in) cake

20cm (8in) cake

35cm (14in)

30cm (12in)

25cm (10in)

20cm (8in)

A/D

Follow C for 3 pillars,
C + D for 6 pillars

35cm (14in)

30cm (12in)

25cm (10in)

35cm (14in)

30cm (12in)

25cm (10in)

20cm (8in)

B

C

35cm (14in)

30cm (12in)

25cm (10in)

20cm (8in)

35cm (14in)

30cm (12in)

25cm (10in)

20cm (8in)

B

C

35cm (14in)   30cm (12in)   25cm (10in)   20cm (8in)

A

A

20cm (8in)   25cm (10in)   30cm (12in)   35cm (14in)

Follow A or B for 4 pillars,
A + B for 8 pillars

D

D

20cm (8in)

25cm (10in)

30cm (12in)

35cm (14in)

20cm (8in)

25cm (10in)

B

20cm (8in)

25cm (10in)

30cm (12in)

35cm (14in)

B

20cm (8in)

25cm (10in)

30cm (12in)

35cm (14in)

A/C

20cm (8in)

25cm (10in)

30cm (12in)

35cm (14in)

USEFUL ADDRESSES

cake decorating supplies

Continental Chef Supplies
Tel 0808 100 1777
www.chefs.net

Copper Gifts
www.coppergifts.com

Divertimenti
Tel 0870 129 5027
www.divertimenti.co.uk

Lakeland
Tel 01539 488100
www.lakelandlimited.com

Little Venice Cake Company
Tel 020 7486 5252
www.lvcc.co.uk

Squires Shop
Tel 0845 225 5671
www.squires-shop.com

Sugar Shack
Tel 0800 597 5097
www.sugarshack.co.uk

Surbiton Art and Sugarcraft
Tel 020 8391 4664
www.surbitonart.co.uk

event/wedding planners

Giles Sherlock Event Design
Tel 020 7221 3361
www.gilessherlock.co.uk

Kathryn Lloyd Wedding Design
Tel / Fax 020 7828 5535
www.kathrynlloyd.co.uk

Wedding Bible Company Limited
Tel 01235 532 719
Email
sarah.haywood@weddingbible.
co.uk

florists

Neil Birks
Tel 020 7259 9746 / 07770 881323
Email: neil@nbflowers.co.uk
www.nbflowers.co.uk

Jill Jeffries
The Fresh Flower Company
Tel 01225 744153
www.jilljeffries.co.uk

Jane Packer Flowers
Tel 0845 074 6000
www.janepackerdelivered.com

Paul Thomas
Tel 020 7499 6889
www.paulthomasflowers.co.uk

Mark Upton
Tel. 0208 510 0333
www.theurbanflowerfirm.com

Mary Jane Vaughan
Tel. 0207 385 8400
www.fastflowers.co.uk

ribbons

Barnett Lawson (Trimmings) Ltd
Tel 020 7636 8591
www.bltrimmings.com

V V Rouleaux
Tel 020 7224 5179
www.vvrouleaux.com

venues

Beach Blanket Babylon
Louisa Rogerson
19–23 Bethnal Green Road
Shoreditch
Lonson
E1 6LA
Tel 020 7749 3540
www.beachblanket.co.uk

Claridge's
Carl Chapman
Brook Street
Mayfair
London
W1K 4HR
Tel 020 7409 6308
www.claridges.co.uk

The Connaught
Mark Tucker
Carlos Place
Mayfair
London
W1K 2AL
Tel 020 7314 3536
www.the-connaught.co.uk

The Dorchester
Gareth Bush
Park Lane
London
W1K 1QA
Tel 020 7629 8888
www.thedorchester.com

The Hempel
Justin Odell
31–35 Craven Hill Gardens
London
W2 3EA
Tel 020 7298 9036
www.the-hempel.co.uk

The Landmark
Chris Thompson
222 Marylebone Road
London
NW1 6JQ
Tel 020 7631 8000
www.landmarklondon.co.uk

Lucknam Park
Rachel Hill
Colerne
Near Chippenham
Wiltshire
SN16 0RB
Tel 01225 742777
www.lucknampark.co.uk

RSA
Amanda Mellett
The RSA House
8 John Adam Street
London
WC2N 6EZ
Tel 020 7451 6815
www.the RSA.org/house

Soho Hotel
Angela Mannerson
4 Richmond Mews
London
W1D 3DH
Tel 020 7559 3000
www.firmdale.com

30 Pavilion Road
Sinead Flynn
30 Pavilion Road
London
SW1X 0HJ
Tel 020 7823 9212
www.30pavilionroad.co.uk

Whatley Manor
Thierry Lepinoy
Easton Grey
Malmesbury
Wiltshire
SN16 0RB
Tel 1666 822 888
www.whatleymanor.com

ACKNOWLEDGEMENTS

It is not surprising that I have discovered a passion for designing couture wedding cakes – my mother studied fashion design at art college and my father's ancestors were master enamellers on the canal boats. As such it has been a pleasure and an indulgence to present a collection of cake designs in this book – with the following thanks:

To my publishing team: Jacqui Small for the opportunity: Lesley for the best initiation you could have; Richard for your stunning photography (with so many girls in your life you have certainly captured the essence of each and every cake); Alison for being so persistent and pedantic with your editing; the fabulous Maggie and Bev for your unfaltering support, hard work and commitment; also a special thank you to Sarah Cuttle and Janine Hosegood for the extra shots.

To my fabulous team at Little Venice Cake Company: Christine (Boo) Lee, who assisted with so many of the hand-decorated iced designs; Colin Chih – you so OWN chocolate; and Camilla Casey and Caroline Morgan for making it all run so smoothly. I am proud of you all and enjoy working with such a talented, passionate team.

To the amazing team at Limelight Management – Fiona, Mary, Alison and Leonie.

To the lovely Esther at Chanel, Old Bond Street.

To Paul Reader and Charlotte Holt at Boodles – thank you for boodling me!

It has been an enormous challenge to photograph each and every one of these cakes on location – my immense thanks to the following individuals who generously gave their venues, flowers, props and time to assist with bringing these cakes to life:

STUNNING VENUES – Thomas Kochs (Liebchen) and Mark Tucker at The Connaught; Carl Chapman at Claridge's; Gordon Ramsay and Michelle Chillingworth at Gordon Ramsay's Amaryllis Room at Claridge's; the gorgeous Gareth Bush at The Dorchester; everyone at Beach Blanket Babylon and The Soho Hotel; Rachel Hill at Lucknam Park; Thierry Lepinoy at Whatley Manor; Justin Odell at The Hempel; Chris Thompson at The Landmark; Amanda Mellett at RSA and Sinead Flynn at 30 Pavilion Road.

FABULOUSLY TALENTED FLORISTS – Neil Birks, Paul Thomas, Mark at TUFF, Jill Jeffries, Sue Barnes at Lavender Green, Jamie Aston, Mary Jane Vaughan and Helen at Jane Packer flowers.

PASSIONATE AND PROFESSIONAL WEDDING / EVENT PLANNERS – Kathryn Lloyd, Amanda Sherlock and Germaine Giles (Giles Sherlock Event Design) and Sarah Haywood.

PERFECT PROPS – Thomas Goode, Jones Hire, Great Hire, Osborne and Little, General Trading Company, Lea Doherty, Asprey, Andrew Prince Jewellery

Thank you to all the fashion designers who constantly design and therefore inspire me – especially Amanda Wakeley for your support.

Finally, thank you to my amazing family – Phil, Marlow and George: you make everything worthwhile.